1393
PACIFIC STREET
CAN YOU TAKE IT?

My Memoir in Early Ministry to Assist
All Who Have Been Called into the
Ministry of Jesus Christ

Pastor Renaldo Watkis

CITI OF
BOOKS

CITIOFBOOKS, INC.
3736 Eubank NE Suite A1
Albuquerque, NM 87111-3579
www.citiofbooks.com
Hotline: 1 (877) 389-2759
Fax: 1 (505) 930-7244

Ordering Information:

Quantity sales. Special discounts are available on quantity purchases by corporations, associations, and others. For details, contact the publisher at the address above.

Printed in the United States of America.

ISBN-13:   Softcover   979-8-89391-547-1

                  eBook   979-8-89391-548-8

Table of Contents

Why This Book? i
Foreword. iii
Consider These First. 1
-Prelude-Possessing The Land. 6
Our First Members. 16
Removing Old Beams And Replacing Them With New 17
Installing A New Ceiling And Light Fixture In The Kitchen 18
Building A Restroom For The Women 19
Tackling The Jungle. 20
Installing Parquet Floor Tiles In The Lower Floor Hallway 21
Carpet In The Sanctuary Changed Due To Water Damage 21
Installing New Windows For The Sanctuary 22
Painting The Sanctuary. 24
Installing Ceiling Fans And Air Conditioning. 25
Create An Outdoor Church Sign. 26
Acquired A Piano For The Sanctuary. 27
Bible Study Classes 28
Articles Written 32
Fellowship Time 36
Hymn. 36
Announcements 37
Ministry Of Giving And Receiving – God's Tithes 38
Ministry Of Giving & Receiving – General Offering. 38
Acknowledgement Of Visitors. 38
Selection 39
Call To Salvation/Membership 39
Communion/Anointing Services 40
Some External Approaches To Ministry 40
Tract Distribution On Nostrand/Fulton Streets 41
Christmas Caroling. 43
Christmas Gift Socks 43
Thanksgiving Blessings. 44

Ministering At The Senior Citizen Nursing Home 46
Door To Door Visits 47
F.o.v.a.v. 47
Bowery Missions (Female & Men) 49
Ministered With Pastor Herbert Daughtry At A Penal Institution 52
Tract Distribution With The Bible Study Group............. 53
Performed Several Weddings........................... 54
Techniques.. 58
Approaches 58
District Fellowship With The N.e. Churches 58
Some Of The Creative Outreach Attempts Rooftop Bells....... 60
Coffee House.. 60
Youth Sunday School................................. 61
Computer Fundamental Class........................... 61
Youth Choir... 64
Food Distribution On Pacific Street And The Block Association
President 65
Created Musical Concerts 67
District Cook-Out.................................... 69
Created A Photography Club........................... 70
Good Friday Presentations............................. 71
External Ministries 73

WHY THIS BOOK?

This book was written for several reasons. First, to leave something tangible behind where anyone can learn about some of the struggles and achievements that I encountered during my early days at the Pacific Street Mission. My hope is that it will provide some level of encouragement to anyone, whether in ministry, or not, and that it will help to inspire and motivate all to "press their way" forward. It was written with the young minister in mind. There are several battles that the child of God goes through, and one of them is accepting the call to ministry. Many do not have a 'blueprint' on what follows the acceptance of this great call. So, hearing and reading it from the experiences of others may provide some level of comfort and guidance as they are going through it.

Lastly, this is an endeavor and testament to my mother, Rebeca Watkis, my two sons Ayinde Peter James-Watkis and Andwele Andrew Watkis, and my wife Sandra E. James-Watkis for being there when I needed them, and their continued love and support.

FOREWORD

Pastor Renaldo Watkis, a friend and fellow parishioner of mine for over four decades, has written a profound book on the trials and tribulations of sustaining and maintaining an urban ministry in an economically oppressed Black community in Brooklyn, New York. Pastor Watkis's ministry was an extension of the historic ministry of The House of the Lord Churches under the leadership of the iconic "people's pastor" Reverend. Dr. Herbert Daughtry and Rev. Dr. Karen S. Daughtry.

Daughtry. The book, 1393 Pacific Street: –Can You Take It? is a must-read for all and anyone who wants to minister to our people in struggling, oppressed Black communities.

The Pacific Street Mission was located on two floors of a brownstone, in the Bedford-Stuyvesant section of Brooklyn. Pastor Watkis was an "all-purpose" pastor. Most assuredly, he delivered powerful weekly sermons, often enhanced by his singing and musical talents on several instruments. He responded to community residents and their challenges and took on the racist, greedy capitalist system and its institutions of oppression. He developed a series of creative tracts that were distributed to the people in his beloved community. He attended rallies, demonstrations, and press conferences and did whatever was needed to speak the truth to power and fight against the system. He also paid particular attention to addressing the importance of meeting the individual's needs of the individual in their journey toward personal salvation. On top of all this, he did construction work in the building and established a beautiful garden in the church's backyard.

In addition to all of that, Pastor Watkis is one of the most creative, hardworking, and caring people I have ever met. He is one hundred percent dependable. If he says he is going to do something, you can rest assured it's going to get done. This book captures his spirit and commitment to the liberating gospel of Jesus Christ. Read and enjoy this powerful message on salvation and liberation.

—Charles Barron

CONSIDER THESE FIRST

Within the pages of scripture, the call to ministry came in various ways. To some it came from a prophet giving word to a husband or wife that their son had a calling on him. To another, the calling came through a dream where a vision was given. To another, prayerful hands were laid upon an individual and the pronunciation of ministry was announced. To another, an Angel was sent. Still to another, a simple," follow me" was uttered. Through scripture, God used various ways to call a person into service with him. To this minister, a combination of a dream, a yearning within my spirit and a 'word' came to me calling me into ministry. Ironically, before 'the call,' I always wanted to explain salvation to the common person. I felt at the time that salvation was passively explained to a potential child of God in a weak manner; it was not defined or clarified. The response of, " just pray about it" would be given, without any steps offered. So, I wanted to clearly explain it. However, when I received my call, it wasn't enthusiastically accepted. Reason being, I'd heard the testimony of our national presider emeritus, reverend Dr. Herbert Daughtry's testimony on when he was called. I heard his story of not having the needed funds to feed his daughter and living at a time in financial hardship. I thought at the time "if this is what's being called to the ministry, then I don't want any parts of it". That decision went on for a while till the Lord started calling me to the ministry. I had received several 'notices' along the way. I remember dreaming a dream whereby I approached an angelic being. He didn't say anything to me but just straightened his arm and pointed his finger, I believe, to his right side. When I awoke, I did not get the impression that he was saying "get away from me," but rather that he was pointing the way for me to go. Though perplexed by the dream, it left an indelible charge in my spirit. A charge that God was calling me for something. At the time I was courting my soon-to-be wife Sandra and shared the dream that I had. It was a dream that latched onto my spirit, and I couldn't shake it off. I guess I was running (or trying to run away) from it because I had a sense that once accepting the call, it would mean that several changes would have to take place in my life. Plus, the thought of going through what I heard from our national minister at the time, did not seem appealing to me. So, I was running. Interestingly enough, after I shared the dream with Sandra, her response did not soothe the trouble I was feeling. She said, "Maybe God is calling you to the ministry." Again, that did not make me feel any better.

Another occasion took place when I attended a revival that was conducted by evangelist John Lawrence at our main church. During that time in our church's history, the baptism in the Holy Ghost was very much sought after. Receiving the Holy Ghost with the evidence of speaking in tongues was on most folks' minds during the revival. Evangelist Lawrence, though a very comical person, started each night with prayer at the altar. Well, one night prior to the revival starting I made myself to the altar seeking the baptism of the Holy Ghost. Initially, I was waiting for one of the brothers to come and tarry with me. However, the brother did not come on time. So I went by myself. I stayed at the altar and prayed so hard that my undershirt became drenched with sweat. As the revival began, I took my time going to the altar. I was wet and tired. Nonetheless, and made my way to the altar. Suddenly I felt the call of God in my spirit. Right then and there I said to the Lord, "Lord, if this is you, I want to know without a shadow of a doubt that it is you. Then in what seemed a quick response, the Lord said, "who do you think you are, wanting all this proof." After receiving the response, I set a date to meet with Reverend H. Daughtry to share with him my call and acceptance to the ministry. After recounting the experience to him, his jovial response was, "welcome to the House of the insane." From that time on, ministry has been an exciting venture. However, since accepting the call, and engaging in numerous areas of ministry, it lifts another consideration; how did my wife feel in hearing me accept the call, and what would my decision mean for her, and how would she fit in?

In the interest of staying neutral, let me use the term 'spouse' as I attempt to speak on several areas that a spouse should be aware of and their great place in the call. First, it needs to be understood that if one is called into ministry, the other is called also. The call of God may not have specifically come to you, but you too have a major part to play in it. As a spouse, you can either be supportive or a hindrance and burden to your spouse. The call of God tends to bring with it a certain level of tension, commitment, separation, absorbance of deceit, aloness, perseverance and much sacrifice. A spouse needs to understand that. To the one who has been called, a spouse needs to understand their spouse's mental, spiritual and physical needs. It's been a saying of mine for years now, "capture the mind, and the body will follow." What is meant by that? Well, if the leadership is captured, or the one called is captured, disabled or burdened down in their ministry, progress or advancement will be curtailed. That is why a spouse plays an essential role in being a barrier at times as well as an encouragement in their spouse's mental, spiritual and physical needs and support. Mental, to provide comparison thoughts and opinions. Spiritual to intercede in prayer for the strength and spiritual stability of the spouse. And physical to be there to provide intimate reassurance. All too often, the enemy of our souls throws curveballs in one if not all these areas at leadership. That is why a hedge of protection needs to be set up, and that can be accomplished by a spouse's intervention. A spouse must move in the same capacity as found in II Timothy 4:11, "only Luke is with me. Get Mark and bring him with you, for he is useful in my ministry." A stark difference is shown in Job 2:9

Of all the things I regret that I did not do was to fellowship more with other ministries and other believers. I don't know if being leery of hearing and/or experiencing other approaches by some in the mishandling of the gospel that created a level of distrust and caution in me, or the fact that I just didn't go in that direction that caused that. In retrospect, I'd wish that I had engaged more. Because in doing so, it would have opened the door to learn of other people as well as expose others to me. So, I would encourage an upcoming minister to venture out and not be afraid to learn of others. You may indeed learn and experience other applications of the gospel of Christ. You may experience it being presented in a musical format or a teaching format. You may find that certain application of the gospel carries well when presented in a way different from the customized 'preached word.' You may discover the effectiveness of joke telling and the importance of timing. Imaginary description of certain biblical events may be just what a young person needs to capture their attention. And of course, fellowship outside of your circle builds alliance and creates a network of other ministers, pastors, evangelists, deacons and bishops you can add to your association of friends.

Though this might be one of the spiritual gifts mentioned in I Cor. 12, a pastor/leader must have the ability to look forward and around the corner in anticipation of what may be coming. This position lends itself to the example found in Gen. 41:1-38. Because of the insight the Lord placed on Joseph spirit, he was able to interpret pharaoh's dream. Not only was he able to interpret the dream, but it also sets an important lesson for us to consider. Leadership must be willing and daring to take progressive steps to ensure advancement and stability of the church. In other words, the leader must assess the "signs of the times" and take decisive action to put in place and train people. They must anticipate the current trends of technology and find those who are able to teach it. They must investigate and find those who can educate the body in managing and stabilizing their financial status and also bring before their congregation those who can spiritually and biblically feed the flock. Within my early years of ministry, I heard several discussions shared by clergy of how much they were paid in rendering a revival or how much they received at their anniversary. I believe that this, for some, was an engaging pursuit that led some down a dangerous path. They made what I call, "payment for preaching" something to be desired. This, in and of itself, is a perversion (I believe) of what the work of the ministry should be about. As you read further in this book, I mentioned a past classmate of mine who when knowing that I was in the ministry asked me, "do you make good money?" The Lord does not call anyone into ministry to "make good money." We are called into ministry for God's service! Now if some sort of compensation is given in the form of an offering or a gift or assistance, then that coincides and falls in line with what's written in the scriptures. However, if that is the main pursuit, then something is drastically wrong. Looking at the scriptures the Bible lifts our attention to Tim. 5:17-18, "Let the elders who rule well be considered worthy of double honor, especially those who labor in preaching and teaching; for the scripture says, 'You shall not muzzle an ox while it is treading out the grain,' and 'The laborer deserves his wages.'" The operative word that is used in both verses is 'laborer;' depicting someone who is working in the ministry. Someone who ministers under the umbrella of love for the sheep. As someone who gives an ear to the concerns and pain of the flop. Someone who anoints the head, arms, heart, legs and feet of the congregational members as they come up for prayer. Consider for a moment the contrast found in various other scriptures: I Tim. 3:3, Mt. 19:16-24, Mt. 6:24, I Tim. 6:9-10, Lu. 12:15, Mk 10:23, Jn 12:4-6.

Lastly, a word on having a 'confidant.' I cannot overemphasize the importance of having someone to share your concerns with. That person should not only hear you but provide sound common sense and scriptural advice. The person should be one that you trust to hold information that is vital and personal. The person should be one that has a solid understanding of scriptural matters and who can listen with an ear of wisdom. All too often, ministers don't have that, and so they 'wing it' on their own. But God has made it so that we are suppose to support one another. Therefore, leadership should not feel that they are upholding and managing their burdens by themselves, someone should be there to uphold them that they can rely on.

-PRELUDE-
POSSESSING THE LAND

I would like to jump in here and say that at some point in time, I found myself standing on the corner of Pacific Street and New York Avenues. I stood there looking down Pacific Street and said to myself, "This block belongs to me!" I felt then that it was a declaration to myself that I was going to do all that I could to influence, change and embed myself into the community. One way or the other, Pacific Street was going to learn and hear from me. I never held to the notion that we were going to be a notch in some corners bound by silence. But instead, we would be a viable entity in the neighborhood engaged in the pulse of the community. Now looking back in retrospect, I thought (at the time) that my personality wasn't one bold enough to take on the position that I took. I grew up mild and not exposed to much of anything. But now, finding myself in a position of leadership, I'd have to make and take on certain moves to progress in life and ministry.

©2022

I don't recall the exact year, month, and time, but it had to be around 1982. I figured it was around that time because my wife was pregnant with our first son. A group of us aspiring ministers met at The House of the Lord Church (Brooklyn, NY) in the National Presider's office for a ministry assignment. The Presider at that time was the "People's Pastor," the Rev. Dr. Herbert Daughtry, and when we gathered in his office, we did not know (at least I didn't), what was about to happen. We listened as he told us we were being assigned to the Pacific Street Mission. Please keep in mind that I'm taking great strides in remembering details of what happened approximately 38 years ago. So, I may be a bit off by a year or two. In the office, the following people had to be there because we all ended up at 1393 Pacific Street: Ken, Queen and Sally Gibson, Antione and Larraine Johnson, Roger and Peggy Howell and my wife Sandra and me. There may have been others there also, but I've mentioned the above names because we were the ones who would lead, conduct, and hold services while assisting Roger Howell who was assigned to be the pastor of the mission. Apparently, this new venture didn't bother nor frighten me, nor did I detect any apprehension from my wife. We all assumed the responsibility and made our way to the new location. We were going to be on the Pacific Street Mission. For clarity's sake, the difference between a 'mission' and a 'church' is that within our church' Constitution, a 'church' is a body composed of 10 or more members who have joined and completed their Orientation lessons. So, when a person joins the church once that body has acquired 10 members, they are considered a church. Whereas a mission is a group of church members who have accepted an assignment to go into a new area of the 'vineyard' to continue ministry and hopefully and prayerfully build its membership to the level of becoming a 'church.'

I don't know where it came from, but in retrospect, I must admit I've always stood up for a new challenge. Moreover, it was at that time in my development that I started questioning a number of things I had read in the scriptures. Questions not to challenge God, but questions related to why I didn't see what I read actualized in the lives of the saints. I remember coming to grips with the fact that God does not play 'favorite' with anyone. At that time, this was a biggie for me because within Christendom, many people placed their trust and indeed their lives in certain individuals. And oftentimes, some of those individuals would rise in the ministry to the point whereby some believed that everything centered around them. Then at some point, some folks would start to acknowledge them as some great entity within the church body. However, for this minister, the position and title that I cherish the most is the title, "SERVANT." It is a position that I've come to love simply because I've learned a long time ago, "It's not me, it's God." "No achievements, It's God." "No limelight, it's God." "No wealth, it's God." What I've also come to realize about the Lord is that He gives each one of us a blank check to excel in Him. Each one of us has the opportunity to soar to higher heights and deeper depths in God. The only condition that one needs is to realize that in order to excel in the Lord there is a cost, which is to be steadfast and unmovable. A condition of having a mind that is made up and keeping one's eyes on Jesus. In the midst of a storm, and when everything is collapsing around, the scripture, "Now unto Him who is able to keep you from falling...," should come to bear. As I've stated before, I don't know where this character trait of confronting challenges came from. Perhaps it came from having a mother who made things happen; a woman who came to this strange country in the hopes of bettering herself and providing a better condition for her two sons. As a young child, I always took notice of how she shopped for groceries; how she compared prices between items. Some of my other skills came from watching her cook and clean around the house; a practice she instilled in both my brother and me. Or, perhaps the drive to take on challenges came from observing our current National Presider Emeritus as he demonstrated how a black man should handle responsibilities. Whichever way it came, I'm grateful because that type of character has brought me a long way in understanding the scriptures and realizing that God is able to take a grain of mustard seed and explode it in all areas of a person's life...if we let Him.

 I'm grateful that certain events in my past left an indelible impression in my spirit. One of which was when I attended several 'Pastoral Anniversary' functions. At that time in my life, I had never attended a formal function where all of us came 'decked-out' in our 'fineries.' The events were held in various locations in Brooklyn, and I remember one event that was held in Pennsylvania. We sat at tables with plates, spoons, forks, and knives in front of us. I was not used to seeing black folks gather under those conditions. Someone else may have experienced those settings in their upbringing, but for me, it was a new experience. And what I liked about it was the fact that we (black folks) were the ones being served. We were the ones being catered to. Someone came to our table and took our food orders and asked us which meat, which vegetable, which starch we wanted to eat. I supposed to this day, it often bothers me when I see black folks serving others, specifically whites. It bothers me because I see that often on TV, in the movies, on shows most of the time where there is some level of servitude being done. In old television shows and in the movies, it would be a black servant serving someone else. In times of old this would be seen but not only in times of old, but also in today's times the practice continues. To this minister, I would think it would be of greater enlightenment for us as a people if we saw ourselves in control of the restaurant employing our own servers.

As I've mentioned before, the make-up of the assisting leadership at the Pacific Street Mission consisted of myself and wife Sandra, Ken and his wife Queen, his sister Sally Gibson and Antoine and his wife Larraine Johnson. All of us had a friendly working relationship with each other and at times we would travel to each other's homes for fellowship and a meal. There were constant sessions of laughing and joking with all of us. We were all young and trying our best to live up to the position of what the lifestyle of a minister in Christ ought to be. I don't recall if any one of us (at that time) had ever received any formal training from any seminary school. I suppose we all took with us what we had learned from our National Presider and ran with it. To this present day, his teaching is still with me as I navigate through the very corridors of ministry. Besides the few mentioned, there were also a few members who were assigned to support the ministry at the Pacific Street Mission. We met on each Sunday, and the pastor at the time, Roger Howell, delivered the message. From time to time, the rest of us were given space to deliver the message for a given Sunday. Any formal training that I received came from observing our National Presider each Sunday at 415 Atlantic Ave. and in some cases, attempting to emulate some of the lessons I'd learned while there. For myself, I had come to embrace the prophetic approach to the gospel because what I read in the pages of scripture agreed with what I'd learned while at our main church. What also started developing within me at the time was a critical eye for ministry. In other words, I started noticing too many ministries concerned and focused only on the internal aspects of their church with little to no regard for the outside world. Great emphasis was placed on 'anniversaries,' 'robes,' 'pastoral offerings,' 'choir numbers,' 'Hammond organs,' 'fur coats and hats,' 'tailored suits,' 'who could grunt, cough and spit the best' etc. Yet, little regard was placed for what was happening on the same block of that (particular) church. Hardly any attention was given or taken to challenging any governmental structure to bring about change in their neighborhoods. So, the teachings I'd received at 415 Atlantic Avenue, left an indelible imprint on my spirit to address and challenge some of the ills I saw back then, and even today.

I found Pastor Howell sincere with a good heart. We all respected the fact that he was appointed as the pastor of the Pacific Street Mission and assisted in whatever capacity possible. He held Bible studies and from time to time, we had meetings and updates to some of the ideas he was attempting to implement. On one occasion, he'd suggested an idea and wanted us to contribute funds toward a down payment on a piece of property on the corner of Bedford and Linden Blvd. I think he had the construction of a church building in mind. The idea was quite 'ambitious,' given the fact that there were only a few of us attending the small mission. Needless to say, the suggestion didn't go too far.

The Pacific Street Mission was located in the Bedford Stuyvesant section of Brooklyn in an apartment building where our National Minister Rev. Herbert Daughtry and his wife once lived. The building itself was a three-floor reddish brick building where the first floor had been converted into the 'church space.' On the top floor lived the tenant Junior Roman with his wife and kids. What became our 'fellowship' room was located on the lower level right beneath the sanctuary. There was a kitchen area in the back and one restroom. The backyard itself looked like a small jungle with plant life overrunning everywhere and the door that led out to the backyard either needed to be replaced or needed much repair. The windows in the 'church space,' or sanctuary, were old and did not provide proper insulation during the winter months. So, one could only imagine what took place with the lack of heat on a given Sunday with only a few of us in the building. Yet, with all these challenges, we made the best of it and pressed our way forward.

A few 'fixups' within the mission took place under Pastor Howell's watch. I remember one occasion when it was decided that an extra restroom was needed for the women to use. Though a noble idea, it was met with a certain level of objection and criticism from the main church (415). Perhaps it was because we did not inform them of what we were doing or had done. I don't recall whether the rest room was ever finished, but I do remember having to do some more extensive work on the room after Pastor Howell left the mission. Hopefully, I'll get to speak on that event a little later in my writing. In addition to some of the work that was done on the restroom, work was also needed in various sections of the building; from plumbing to electrical to painting to cementing to plastering to flooring to construction to branch removal to erecting beams to installing a kitchen ceiling and light fixture to installing a kitchen sink with cabinets to laying down carpeting and floor tiles etc. Those events too, I will speak extensively in this book.

At some point, Minister Ken Gibson along with his wife Queen and sister Sally stopped coming to the mission. I really don't know why or what happened. Though gradually several others who were assigned to the mission also left. Whether the Gibson's departure had any bearing on them, remains a mystery to me. Those of us who remained, continued to hold down the fort with the Sunday services, meetings, and Bible studies. One of the things that I would have liked to see happen was for Pastor Howell to inquire of me what and how I was doing in my ministry. I've always felt that it was important for leadership to inquire how one's ministry was going and what they were doing to improve, encourage and support them as they were navigating through ministry. At the time, I had a consistent Bible study going on at my job site. The studies that I conducted went on for several years and some of the participants/people who attended and received Christ as their Savior were old enough to be my grandparents. In fact, one of them (Charlotte Johnson), the oldest in the class, introduced me to CBD (Christian Book Distributors), and encouraged me by giving me several of her books. I would have loved to share with him how the classes started; how at the time I'd asked one of the saints there "Where were the Christians in the facility?," and how I was introduced to some of them. To this day, I still believe that it is vital and important for us to share with our fellow workers what we are doing in our part of the vineyard. To me, it would be encouraging and tie us closer together in faith. However, the flip side of that coin is when one does ministry work without any accountability, interjection, encouragement or guidance from leadership. It may create an atmosphere where an individual "fends for themselves" with unnecessary trials and errors along the way. I suppose that is part of the reason I admire the apostle Paul so much. His mentee was Timothy, and it was this mentee that he took under his wings to mentor him in the areas of ministry. It was his mentee Timothy which he encouraged to stay the course and to also stir up the gift that was placed on him. In the reading of the text, Paul reminded Timothy not to allow anyone to belittle and look down upon him because of his youth. Paul spent time guiding and instructing his protégé in the different challenges and aspects of ministry. And in my humble opinion, that may be one of the crucial voids that continue to happen today; not having a mentor to guide a young student. From my recollection, no one had joined the church in the space of time we were there.

In the East New York section of Brooklyn, a community room had become available and because of the work and notoriety of our National Presider, the space was made available to the House of the Lord for the rental cost of $1.00 a year. From what I understood, they couldn't give the space away free, so they charged us $1.00 a year. In a short while, Min. Antione Johnson and his wife Laraine Johnson assumed the leadership in that area of East New York. The facility was very spacious and had fully functional restrooms for both male and female, along with a large kitchen area. As chairs were set up, there was plenty of space around to conduct Sunday school classes or any other set-up that one wanted to create. Meanwhile, at the Pacific Street Mission, Pastor Howell and his wife Peggy eventually left the mission.

Now with the space once again inactive and empty, a Family Night church meeting was held at our main church on Atlantic Avenue. On the agenda was the Pacific Street Mission; what was to come of it. During the discussion, with most of the church membership in attendance, Minister Ronald Stone suggested something that would steer my life in a path that would broaden my development as a minister in the gospel of Christ. "Why don't we ask Minister Watkis what he wants to do?" Pastor Howell was no longer there, Minister Gibson had left, and Minister Johnson was gone. A choice was given. A choice for me to come back to 415 and resume pulpit duties on a Sunday, or a chance to chart in a new direction by assuming the leadership of the Pacific Street mission. Well, I chose the latter. I thought at the time, pulpit assignments were redundant, and I didn't see any growth in that. It was a great challenge, but I decided to accept the challenge to go forth. I don't even think I'd asked my wife for her opinion; I just accepted the challenge.

What should be noted here is that we were not the first ones to start a mission at 1393 Pacific Street, nor was this the church's first attempt to start a mission. Our church has had a history of starting other churches and missions in various states. Beaver Falls, Pennsylvania; Augusta, Georgia; Washington DC; Raleigh NC and Jersey City are a few places where missions were successfully planted. However, the mission at 1393 Pacific Street saw various pastors in the course of its history. Our National Presider Rev. H. Daughtry developed and continued his ministry there. But besides him, there was Telford Pearce, Jimmy Robinson, Roger Howell and then me. Others like Dorothy Isaac and Barbara Williams came later, after me. What I found interesting was that the others mentioned before me all started with a congregation. They all had people occupy the seats and pews in the small sanctuary of Pacific Street, but I didn't. When I assumed the leadership of the Pacific Street mission, the only people there at the time were my wife Sandra and my two young sons Ayinde and Andwele. Since that time, I've come to learn that those conditions were what I needed to mold me into what I've become today. In addition, all who I've previously mentioned (Telford Pearce, Jimmy Robinson, Roger Howell, Dorothy Isaac and Barbara Williams) are no longer with us today. Some have made their transition, while others have moved on. I supposed the elders had it right when they stated, "hindsight is 20/20," because in retrospect, I now understand and thank God for the experiences I've learned there. I don't believe that the experiences I've garnered could have come from no other than to go through what I went through at the Pacific Street Mission. Oftentimes, I found myself going through a deep search within my soul and spirit to come to an understanding and settlement that not only was the experience part of ministry, but that I had to stay the course and complete what God had placed on my life. The glamor of robes and a certain prestige was not part of it. Nor was the amount of an anniversary or speakers offering the determining factor. I had to know beyond a shadow of a doubt that God called me into ministry, and that I had examples of men and women who went through (and more), the same trials that I went through.

So now, I was challenged with the responsibility to start a ministry with what I had. There was no one to usher; no one that I could call on to do a solo; not even a clean-up committee to set up the chairs and clean up after we were finished. Those responsibilities were solely left up to my wife and me. In addition to who and what weren't there, was the challenge to build a congregation within the community where the mission was located. Still, another major challenge was the church space itself. The sanctuary, the pulpit area, the lower hallway floor, the Fellowship room, my little office space, the kitchen area and the restroom, all needed work. Some areas needed more work than others while one area in particular, the kitchen floor, was upheld by the grace of God. Termites had completely eaten out the beams that supported the floor in the kitchen. I will speak about that later.

Now, be it far from me to put most of what you're reading into any type of chronological sequence. That is not going to happen! There may be some points that I link together, but most of it will be experiences that happened and my thought process that followed at that particular time. The idea here is to share experiences that could aid any minister coming up the ranks of ministry. We oftentimes have a fantasy of grandeur when we see leadership on a pulpit expounding on the Word or wearing some colorful weaved robe. We tend to do that. A great event would happen, and we would get lost in the final product. A preacher would deliver and break down the word, and we get lost in the "hoop-n-holla." Yet we fail to comprehend the length of time and energy that the minister sacrificed in study and preparation. We only see the final product or outcome. From the time of Pacific Street to the present, I've taken notice from my own experience (and the experiences of others) that the 'word,' or the message will not always come at a time where it gives the minister some "wiggle room" to prepare. There will be times when the preached word will come at the 'ninth hour.' And this is where the ability to draw on what was learned before in prior readings and deliverances comes into play. A minister has to be poised and confident enough to stand before a congregation and deliver the word.

Let me insert here also the appreciation for the teaching of the 'old-school' which taught us to thank God and to be an observant student. I would often say to folks, "before the old school disbanded, I attended the last class." In my opinion, there is a grave danger when assimilation takes place within the body, doctrine and spirit of the church; so much so, that we are now entertaining lifestyle issues, doctrinal standards and mocking the Spirit of God. I understand 'changing times,' but the Word of God doesn't change, and when we compromise it, we will find ourselves walking on very thin ice. From what I've read in scripture, the Lord has a standard that every one of us must measure up to. Sometimes I feel as if humanity creates cultures and laws and then expects God to follow them. Or, by our impulses and desires, we expect the Lord to 'take the witness stand, raise his hand and give an account to tell the truth, the whole truth and nothing but the truth.' In other words, it's not what the Lord commands of us, it's what we demand of God; and that is to accept our idols and the lifestyles that fit us. Wrong move!

Part of what I've also learned from the 'old school' is to stick to it until the job is done. Too many throw in the towel after a 'minute.' They tend to start off with gusto, then after the trials and tribulations come, they give up and quit. They may have started off with great fanfare, then after the dust settles, and the work that's demanded of them piles up, they give up and quit. But thank God for such scriptures as: Matt 10:22 "And ye shall be hated of all *men* for my name's sake: but he that endureth to the end shall be saved." John 6:27 "Labour not for the meat which perisheth, but for that meat which endureth unto everlasting life, which the Son of man shall give unto you: for him hath God the Father sealed." 1Cor 13:7 "Beareth all things, believeth all things, hopeth all things, endureth all things." The key word that stands out in all three verses (Mt. 10:22, Jn. 6:27, 1Cor. 13:7) is the word '**ENDURETH.**' In other words, come hell or high water, keep your hands on the plow and forge ahead. You may stumble and fall, and that's okay, but get back up and keep on 'trucking,' keep on building, keep on planning, keep on dreaming, keep on trying, keep on writing, keep on strategizing, keep on applying, keep on studying. Just keep on!

That is the lesson that I also learned from my mom 'Becky.' She came here (U.S.) from Colon, Panama as a young woman, and kept on struggling. She worked day and night until her breakthrough came through. At a young age, I witnessed how she labored tirelessly providing for her two sons and often worked the 'graveyard' shift to put a roof over our heads and food on the table. Brought up a devout Catholic, her faith in God never wavered, and still within the confines of the house in which she completely purchased, and where we now live, there remain remnants of a relationship she had with the Lord.

Looking back in retrospect however, I'd taken on the responsibility of leading the mission, but I thank God my wife hung in there with me because neither one of us knew what was in store. Pacific Street had many challenges. Not only the challenge of the building itself, but the community and its surroundings as well. Two blocks away on the corner of Atlantic and Bedford Avenues, stood the Armory – one of several in the Brooklyn area. Somewhat of a shelter, it provided housing and meals for the less fortunate. A block away from the mission were several multi-level apartment buildings. The neighborhood had its share of low-income tenants, with some who hung outside of the local liquor stores. On a given weekend, you could find many of the kids on the block playing together and from time to time, they had their disagreements, but shortly thereafter, their playing continued.

OUR FIRST MEMBERS

One day while I was at the mission, a gentleman came into the sanctuary, sat down and started sharing his desire to find a church he and his wife could attend. He stated that he had been looking for a place of worship and noticed ours. His name was Marcus Sergeant. Soon after that, he brought his wife, Celithia Sargeant. Born in St. Vincent, they both had moved into the area on St. Marks Street and were looking for a place to worship. I had informed him that we were a small congregation and were looking to work within the community to build the mission. Not long after our initial meeting, they both attended our services and became members of the Pacific Street mission. However, I found it fascinating to see that after a while of attending, his attendance dwindled a bit while his wife steadily continued. Later, I found out that he was in need of employment. He did not mention any specialized trade or skills that he had, he just needed to find a job. On my job, I went to the Housekeeping Dept. and spoke to the director of the department to see if he could do anything for me. He then told me to ask brother Sargeant to come in and fill out some papers. Soon after that, brother Sargeant became a member of the Housekeeping Department at Coler Memorial Hospital. I was very glad that I was placed in a position to help and assist our first member. But it also raised another important lesson for me, and the lesson is, "When you have a good reputation, it will open doors for you." In other words, when anyone carries themself in a good manner; when anyone conducts business in a proper manner, it speaks volumes. The director of housekeeping more than likely knew me from the way I interacted with the Administration Department. He probably saw me opening up an event in prayer or speaking on behalf of my coworkers. Something must have inspired him (for him) to grant me my appeal to employ Mr. Sargeant. I think I've conducted myself enough in a manner that captured the attention of those around me while employed in the hospital. And by my manner of behavior, some may have deduced that I had a respectable disposition. They may have taken notice of the way I articulated myself, or the crowd with which I associated myself with. A good reputation may have 'cracked the door open' for me to reach and touch the housekeeping supervisor's heart, which made it easier for him to grant me my request. So, I truly believe that a good reputation had something to do with it.

REMOVING OLD BEAMS AND REPLACING THEM WITH NEW

As I've mentioned before, the building itself required a lot of work. One of the first areas we tackled was the kitchen floor. Upon inspection of the basement beams, I found out that the floor of the kitchen was being supported by the 'grace of God.' Termites had completely eaten through much of the corner wooden ends that went through the bricks on both sides of the wall. Luckily, not too many people stayed in the kitchen area before or after the services. The beams required immediate attention and needed to be replaced. Thank God that 'Junior,' the tenant that lived on the top floor volunteered to assist me in replacing the beams. What I liked about that brother was the fact that he had a 'willing and generous' spirit." He rolled up his sleeves and was not looking for anything in return. As a matter of fact, much of the heavy work that was performed at the mission was assisted by him. I could not have envisioned myself removing any old beams, but he could. To me, it seemed like another expense that we could not afford. But through his willingness and determination to do it, the work started.

On one occasion while I was heading down to the church (415 Atlantic Ave.) on a snowy day, I took notice of some street construction work that was being done. It may have been B.U.G., or perhaps Con Edison who had created some trenches in the street area. I also noticed that there were fresh beams of wood that were being used to build a wall barrier for the workers to do their work. Well, long story short, as I passed by, I stopped my Hyundai Excel and inquired from one of the workers whether I could have a beam or two from their pile. Once I heard, "Help yourself," that was all I needed. Two of the long beams were shoved into the back of my Hyundai and made its way to 1393 Pacific Street. Once arriving there, the wood was shoved through our Fellowship Room window and stayed there until it dried.

Once dried, Junior and I went to work. We were able to take out the rotted beams and replace them with fresh ones. Being a mechanic by trade, Junior brought in a transmission jack to lift up the flooring as the new beams were installed. The transmission jack was strategically placed in the basement and pumped while a section of the flooring was lifted and set in place. Thank God for Junior. While the process was being done, the sound of wood cracking was a bit concerning, but I understood that by the repositioning and elevation of the floor, that sound would happen. Plywood was purchased and used for the flooring section that was replaced. Before long, the kitchen floor was done!

INSTALLING A NEW CEILING AND LIGHT FIXTURE IN THE KITCHEN

With the flooring done, the next area where work was needed was the kitchen ceiling. The ceiling itself had cracks and small holes which I thought needed to be 'patched-up.' I remember calling in a construction person to get an estimate of how much it would cost to 'patch-up' the ceiling. The person said that he would remove the old ceiling and replace it with a new one. Well, all I saw at the time was another expense. But after he made that suggestion and left, the thought came to mind, "we could do that work ourselves." It should be understood that our budget at that time was very limited. The previous pastor did not leave us with much funds to use, plus the necessary fix-ups that were done for other areas of the church required that the limited funds be used. So, money was not in abundance. In addition, I recalled going to our main church to ask for assistance. However, the level of assistance did not come as I'd expected it to. So, we managed with what we had, went into our own personal treasury, and developed some creative ways to raise the funds that were needed. I do not know if I (have) mentioned it already, but Weissman Salvage was the store where most of the purchases were made to fix up our mission. From doors to lumber to windows to cabinets-Weissman Salvage was the place. After several panels of sheetrock were purchased along with a lighting fixture, the work began. I solicited some of the female members from our main church and they rolled up their sleeves and came down to give me a hand. Thank God for our sisterhood! The entire old ceiling was removed and made ready for the new. However, once the work began, helpers were not readily available to help, especially when the time came for lifting and holding up one end of the sheet rock. So, while there, I had to devise a way to get that done. Throughout the years there on the mission, several obstacles had to be addressed without the help and assistance of others. And I thank God that He gave me a creative mind to address them. In reconstructing part of the kitchen ceiling, I devised a supporting way to prop up one side of the sheetrock with a plank of wood, while lifting, holding, and fastening the other end with my drill. It worked! Once the ceiling was in place, a lighting fixture with a pull string was installed.

BUILDING A RESTROOM FOR THE WOMEN

The next area of work was finishing the restroom for the women. In the lower floor area, only one restroom was available, and it did not feel right having everyone use the same restroom. So, plans and designs went into effect to create a restroom for the sisters to use; a project 'easier said than done.' I cannot personally speak of any formal training that I'd received or any schooling I undertook to learn anything about construction, architecture, design, modeling, measurements, carpeting or plumbing. Nor did I know of any training that our top floor tenant Junior received. All that I know is that the Lord made a way! It kind of reminds me of how God gives some a 'Word of Knowledge' and a 'Word of Wisdom' in creating certain things; I supposed the same way He spoke to Noah in creating the ark. As a minister embarking in ministry, I had to have enough faith to see this.

Now with the limited space available, the design of the room had to accommodate not only a toilet for use, but a sink as well. There also had to be enough space so that we could make our way to the backyard when needed as well as come into the kitchen area. The tenant Junior went to work installing the piping for the waste line, and we also installed the walls, small sink and reinforced the door that led to the backyard.

TACKLING THE JUNGLE

Though the backyard was not a large area, it required a lot of work. One would think that a small area does not need too much attention to upkeep, but removing plants from the ground with their branches and leaves growing everywhere is a monumental task. It not only required tools, but manpower as well. The neglected space required sweeping, raking, cutting, boxing and bagging all that would be slated for sanitation. Brothers Booker Green and Jerry King, along with my two sons Ayinde and Andwele provided the assistance and help that I needed. Though we never utilized the area, it was still a good idea (for cosmetic sake) to get it cleaned up.

INSTALLING PARQUET FLOOR TILES IN THE LOWER FLOOR HALLWAY

Even though I have always been intrigued by some level of construction, I have come to discover that it would help if more than one person were doing it all. The fascination of seeing what others may have called 'broken,' and envisioning what could be built inside, in back and around was always intriguing to me. But again, some manual laborers are best enjoyed and appreciated when others are there to assist and help. I supposed in the years of neglect, some of the physical structure at 1393 Pacific Street just withered and decayed. Part of which had to do with the flooring in the lower floor. The wood was old and dry, so parquet tiles were purchased and installed on the floor. However, amid the measuring, cutting and installing the tiles, knee pads were not worn and as a result, one of my knees became inflamed with fluid in the joint, which made it difficult for me to squat or even kneel. I still remember going to see a doctor and the long needle he used to extract the fluid from my knee. Little did I know that my journey of being called into God's ministry would entail this kind of 'training.' Well, the work was started and completed with a sense of pride. And knowing that anyone going from our sanctuary to the Fellowship Room, kitchen or restroom would encounter a brand-new flooring that was painstakingly installed with much determination and pride.

CARPET IN THE SANCTUARY CHANGED DUE TO WATER DAMAGE

Looking back in retrospect, it had to be God who kept me going in the midst of all the 'fixups' that had to be done. I did not like the thought of inviting anyone to the mission with all the broken pieces that had to be fixed. If someone came to our service and had to use the restroom, my thought would be, "What will they see or smell down there?" Water, as innocent as that substance is, created more mold in the lower basement where the furnace was and probably aided in the rotting of the beams (along with the termites), in the kitchen area. Water also caused the flooring in what we used as the front of the sanctuary to warp. Water, coming from several areas of the sanctuary, caused parts of the wall to crumble. All those areas had to be addressed by fixing them. But the main area was the flooring itself. So again, we dipped into our treasury to purchase plywood to line the entire front part of the pulpit. Again, I should state here that whatever funds that had been left from the previous leadership were used to purchase what we needed to get the job done. Thank God some of us had the wherewithal to fix things because had we contracted a plumber, electrician, painter, or construction company, it would have run us thousands of dollars (which we did not have) to get the job done. So, with the purchase and transport of plywood from the lumber yard, work began, and we were able to fortify the floor. Addressing a warped floor was not a straight-cut deal of just laying plywood down. Special cuts were needed to fit around the radiator and heating pipes that ran from the floor to the ceiling. Thank God we were able to secure carpet squares to fill most of the area around the pulpit. I should also state that the carpet squares were a small part of the donation that we were able to get from the Health and Hospital Corporation. Hopefully, I will get a chance to share how that blessing unfolded.

INSTALLING NEW WINDOWS FOR THE SANCTUARY

I think I may have mentioned earlier in my writing that the windows inside the sanctuary were old and some of the glass broken. During the winter months, it became more and more challenging maintaining heat in the sanctuary. I can recall at one point, smoke coming out of my mouth as I stood in the pulpit area. Under those conditions, we had to take drastic steps to rectify the problem. But one major obstacle was ever in our way--finances. We simply did not have the finances to cover buying windows for the sanctuary. Nor did we have the expertise or person to install them. I could not at the time figure out how we were going to secure new windows for the place.

Minister Alice B. Edwards used to sing a song, "May the work that I've done speak for me." Those lyrics are so true because the life that we as Christians live speaks volume to those looking on/at us. And oftentimes, we are not aware that people are 'watching' us. With each action that we take, someone is watching us. The language that we use, someone is listening to us. Whether we know it or not, someone is taking note of what we are doing as Christians. That is why we ought to do our best to exemplify the Christ in us. We may not reach it all the time, but we ought to try.

Living right next door to the mission lived a Haitian brother by the name of Femille. On one occasion while we were there at the mission, Femille came outside his house in what seemed to be his pajamas and said hello to me. In our brief exchange, Femille suggested changing the windows in the sanctuary. It was a suggestion that he raised out of the blue. But the icing on the cake came when he stated that he would install the windows for me. He did not mention any charge for the work, but only that he saw what I was trying to do in the building. He took notice of some of the renovations and fixups that were taking place, and he wanted to help.

With the need for windows and the lack of funds, I must have shared the concern with my aunt, Deacon Betty Brazell, and she eventually responded with, "Don't worry about it. We will get people to sponsor a window in the name of a loved one." If that was not a stroke of genius, I don't know what was. She sponsored a window along with three other saints from our main congregation. In no time flat, my financial concerns were quickly dismissed in a matter of days by the generous help and contribution of my fellow Christian family. In addition, Weissman Salvage provided me with four brand new double pane windows to insulate our sanctuary.

When Femille started the work, he came out in pajamas again and started tearing out the rotted wood and frame. Without a care in the world, he swung his hammer and broke out all the pieces in the frame of the window. I must confess, at that time the thought did cross my mind whether he could do the job. After all, I did not have any working references about him or whether he knew what he was doing. I only went on blind faith. Before long, I was looking at a huge empty hole in the wall. He then needed some additional material to secure the first window, so I found myself going to a local hardware shop on Nostrand Avenue to buy the additional pieces. One of the things that I did while working at Coler Memorial Hospital, was watch when certain workers used their expertise around the hospital. I wanted to know how certain things were fixed. So, I asked questions, and because I had a good rapport with the guys, they would supply me with information and some parts that I needed. As I watched Femille knock out the frame and install two front windows, it gave me the confidence to 'try it' for myself. The windows were put in place and secured and in an instant, we could feel the difference in the sanctuary. The seepage of air that came through the front windows during the winter months was over. New windows have been installed!

Not too long after the installation of the front windows, I decided to tackle the two back windows by myself. Unfortunately, Weissman Salvage did not have the same length windows as the front, so I had to improvise a bit to install the back ones. Within my mind I thought, "if certain things did not fit properly, I would find a way to 'make it work." I remember seeing Femille swing his hammer a certain way. So, I did the same. Before long, a third hole had been created in the back of the sanctuary and a new window was installed. Thank God for talents and the willingness to venture outside of my comfort zone. Now after installing all the windows, the sanctuary felt like a different place…with heat during the winter.

PAINTING THE SANCTUARY

Our work continued with painting the sanctuary. For this task, I evoked some wisdom knowing that additional help would be needed for the venture of putting a new coat of paint on the sanctuary walls. I requested the help of some of the brothers from our main church (415) and they assisted me in the project. Some of the brothers included: Keith Johnston, Kenneth Smith, Bud Revels and Brother Bertrum. Prior to painting the sanctuary walls, I had done some dabbling in that kind of work before. So, with prior knowledge, it made it easier to know what paint and brushes to buy. The brothers came in, and we divided the sanctuary into sections and went to work. I really appreciated them for taking their time to help and assist me with the project. Please keep in mind, at that particular time in our mission's history, we did not have any male membership to call on; this is not to say that the women could not do the work. Some of the sisters played a pivotal part in our "Outreach Ministry," which I will expound on later in this writing.

INSTALLING CEILING FANS AND AIR CONDITIONING

I have always held the belief that "it does not make any sense to beautify a church building or sanctuary if nobody is visiting it." However, in the interim of waiting for the people to come, I also believed that the sanctuary of the Lord needed to be a place where one not only could find 'comfort' but be 'comfortable' while attending the service itself. So, we installed a ceiling fan to cool off the sanctuary. I never was one to put too much stock into beautifying a sanctuary. In some places, hundreds if not tens of thousands of dollars were spent in putting up ornaments, statues, paintings, pictures, chandeliers, lighting, special pews, pulpit furniture and so on. Though the house of God should not look empty and worn down, I believe that it should be designed with the thought of worshipping and praising God. Too much 'stuff' to me can be a bit distracting. An attempt was later made to install a window air conditioner, however, what we discovered was that because of the old wiring, the current from the air conditioner was too strong to use in that section of the building. Each time the unit was used, the power in the sanctuary went out. Several trips were made to the basement to replace blown out fuses. Eventually, I scrapped the effort, and we only used the ceiling fan.

CREATE AN OUTDOOR CHURCH SIGN

Each Sunday we met at the mission for services. Along the way, we acquired another member Sister Cheryl Ledlum, who joined us with her young daughter Nefertiti. I had met Sister Ledlum through Amway. We both were involved with that organization as we were trying to build a clientele list in the community to sell cleaning products. On each Sunday, we would enter the building and have services, but there was no 'identifier' outside the building to let the community know that we were even there. So, an interesting thing happened one day when I went from the job site to buy lunch during my lunch break. While waiting for my order, a truck with sheets of metal plates almost caused an accident. The metal bands that secured the sheets broke, and the sheets flew off the flatbed of the truck. Amazingly, no one got hurt. It was a dangerous situation, but it also turned into a God sent opportunity. Right there on the spot, the thought came to my mind that we could use one of those sheets to make our church sign. So, I approached the driver and asked what was to become of the sheets, and whether I could have one of them. When he gave me the 'green light,' I somehow managed to roll up and secure one of the metal sheets and put it in the back of my car.

From Coler Memorial Hospital where I worked, I made myself back at 1393 Pacific Street. Now I have a new project--create our church sign.

The metal sheet was taken downstairs into our Fellowship Room and stretched out on one of the tables. There were no visible signs of dents because great care was taken in preventing that. So, with the purchase of strips of wood and paint, work began on designing and constructing our church sign. I've always liked the idea of 'fellowshipping' with the saints. I felt that early in my ministry, we as a body of believers needed to fellowship more than just waiting for a national meeting to take place. So, the name that I gave the Pacific Street mission was, "The House of the Lord Fellowship Center" (at that time we did not have a visible sign outside of the building). Since artistic endeavors were part of my background, the talent was used in painting and designing our church sign. As I am writing this, I am trying to recollect how we managed to put up the sign outside. I vaguely remember standing on the very top of a shaky ladder we had and anchoring the ends to the outside wall while holding on to the metal bars of the window. In retrospect, a number of things we were able to accomplish at the mission really surprised me. I can't really understand where the drive came from to do all those things but thank God that He gave us the persistence to accomplish them. Now, with our 'identifier' in place, the community knew that there was a place they could go to for worship and fellowship.

ACQUIRED A PIANO FOR THE SANCTUARY

As I sit here in my office putting this book together, I thank God for the ability to type. That learning came from a place where I attended back when I was in my early twenties. The place was called O.I.C., which is the acronym for 'Opportunities Industrialization Center.' Somehow, I got involved in that organization and learned how to type, file and so on. Well, I, being a friendly fellow, one day while talking with a classmate about music and church, she stated that her family had an upright piano that they wanted to get rid of. So again, like the sheets of metal that flew off the truck, I said to her, "Well why not give it to me? We could use a piano in our mission." Surprisingly she said, "Okay." Which brings me to another lesson taught within the scriptures, "You have not, because you ask not." Simply stated, many Christians don't have because they don't ask, or may feel that what they are asking for is outside of their scope of faith to ask.

I'm sure it was a relief to her and her family to get rid of the piano, and a blessing and relief for us to get it. I then acquired the help and muscle of some of our brothers and we transported the piano from her house to the mission. I was not concerned whether the unit needed tuning or not. That was the easy part. What concerned me was how we were going to lift that heavy instrument from the street level, up a number of stairs into the sanctuary. But with the will and determination of all, we got it done! Once placed in its permanent spot, a piano tuner was asked to come and fine tune our 'brand new/used' piano. Once again, the Lord showed Himself in this miracle.

BIBLE STUDY CLASSES

During my tenure at the mission, I started several Bible studies. I suppose that it was at that time in ministry that I started delving deeper and took on a questionable attitude toward the scriptures. I've always stated that the Word of God is like a 'smorgasbord' to me. When read, there is a plethora of information, insight, discoveries, understanding and sense all taking place at the same time. And the thing that I sought most was applying 'spiritual sense' to it all. In other words, it is still my belief that when one applies worldly understanding to the Word of God, it simply will not work. The word of God must be viewed from a spiritual perspective. To come from a human standpoint or understanding will fail all the time! Perhaps that is why the Word of God instructs us that, "God is a Spirit, and they that worship Him must worship Him in Spirit and in Truth." (John 4:24) God is not a human. His make-up is not flesh and blood. His movements are not like ours. And His wisdom is far beyond human comprehension.

As I have stated, several Bible studies were conducted in various places. One of the first places that I started my study was in Coler Memorial Hospital with some of the saints who worked there. It was interesting how it all developed. While in the early years of working there, I remembered asking one of the saints whom I met (Sister Lula Bradley), where I could find the rest of the Christians who worked in the institution. She directed me to the Protestant Chapel. She stated that some of the saints congregated there during their lunch hour for prayer. So, I went and grafted myself in with some who were then my seniors at the time. There was Sister Marie Cooper, Brother Alfredo Gonzales, Sister Charlotte Johnson, Sister Denise Colon, Sister Lucille Nelson and of course, Sister Lula Bradley. As we continued with the prayer meetings, the day came when I felt it necessary to go a bit further and introduce starting a Bible study with them. I felt so honored that all allowed me to conduct a Bible study with them. However, in starting the study, I was very mindful to teach just the Bible and not interject some of the radical positions that I've learned from the 'House.' I felt that in doing so, I would lose some of them. I have found that many Christians (in my opinion), are very narrow minded in their faith walk with God. We can have a 'hoop -n-holla' time in church, but when the dust settles, we don't know one thing about who to call when our streets need cleaning, or when the police mistreat (or kill) one of our friends or family members, or the business and use of politics. All that most folks come away with is that they had a great time in service. So, I taught 'straight' Bible.

I could go into many experiences I had with the class, but suffice it to say, I will lift only a few of them. Sister Charlotte Johnson was the oldest who attended our class. And the one thing that stood out about her was the fact that she was the most enthusiastic, responsive, and studious one in the class. I should also state here that she received the Lord while attending our Bible study class. She introduced me to C.B.D. (Christian Book Distributors), a Christian book supplier and also furnished me with many of her own books. It was my honor of not only sharing the Word of God with them, but also introducing, or perhaps exposing them to other study aides to guide them along their path of salvation. Till this day, I have shared study aides such as Bible Commentaries, Bible Atlas, Bible Dictionaries, Bible Concordance and various versions of other Bibles to the people of God. Others within the class like Sister Bradley and Brother Gonzales were very helpful, encouraging, and supportive to me during the many years of conducting the sessions. Some of whom I have mentioned have gone on to receive their reward from the Lord: Sister Marie Cooper, Sister Lucille Nelson, Sister Charlotte Johnson, Brother Alfredo Gonzales, Sister Denise Colon and Sister Roslyn Woods-McCalla. I bless God for their support and patience in what took place years ago.

Another study that took place happened at the home of my aunt Deacon Betty Brazell. "Tuddy," as she was affectionately called, was all of the above; 'inspiring,' 'supportive,' 'enthusiastic,' 'encouraging,' 'welcoming,' 'hospitable' and more! When the thought arose of starting a study at her home, she ran with it and started the process. Neighbors were invited to the sessions and after each session, we all sat and ate together. Little did I know that in the early stages of some of those studies, I was honing my understanding, knowledge, and skills of teaching study classes. There was a brief study that started at the home of Sister Sharman Blake. It did not go on for too long, but from there, another was started in the Bronx. Though I cannot recall whose home we visited at the time. Right within the mission itself, a Bible study was conducted as we made several attempts to galvanize people in the community to attend. The response of the community was little to none. But my teachings encouraged me to press on despite what 'I thought I saw or didn't see.' Bible studies were also started with the Brotherhood of the House (415), as well as with the general membership. With the Brotherhood, I recall one instance where once in the class, a brother tried to interject a deviation from our subject study to something else. It reminded me of a time when a sister within the Bible study at Coler Memorial (Sis. P. Cato), accepted the Lord into her life. After that took place, I checked on her several days after and noticed that she had a book on her desk that dealt with some other beliefs. My instruction and encouragement to her was for her to first build up her own faith in Christ, then once reaching that, she then could be at a place of reading and understanding other beliefs and faiths in relation to her own. In other words, for a person who just came into the saving grace of Christ, I do not think it is wise for them to take up other persuasions, ideologies, concepts, beliefs or even faiths. That is not going to strengthen a person in his or her own faith in Christ. But rather, it would be wiser for that person to know who Christ is, and who they are in Him. Amen? So once the brother attempted to shift our study in another direction, I stopped it and redirected us back on course of our study. Leadership must always be aware of that which can cause confusion to the body, especially when the souls of individuals are involved.

Throughout the years, I've been a student who takes note of what's going on, and how to address certain circumstances. On that note, I recall an instance where a speaker came into our congregation and shared some things that were not consistent with scripture. The national presider (at the time) Pastor H. Daughtry stood up as soon as the speaker finished and sternly corrected what was said to the congregation. In another instance, an evangelist was invited to preach and made an outlandish suggestion; that if two Christians engaged in a certain moral sin, the punishment would not be as severe. Well, needless to say, that person was never invited to speak again. For the spiritual wellbeing of the congregation, leadership must from time to time, step in and correct, rebuke, chastise and safeguard the congregation from erroneous teachings and practices by others. If the teaching and preaching is contrary to the scriptures, then the leader must have the God given boldness to stop it!

Within the general Bible study that was held with the membership, I thought it would be interesting to implement several challenges that would make the class fun. So, I invented "Pass the Peas." That was a fun way to engage the attendees to pass a sock filled with peas from one member to another as each one attempted to answer Biblical questions. Another was a Bible trivia game that someone gave me several years ago. A little red plastic box contained questions from both the Old and New Testaments. Still, another was the 'pop-up' tests that took place from time to time, or the definition of certain Biblical words, or the cross-matching of words with their meaning. I even went as far as to create a wooden rectangular box with circular covered holes and a toggle cord with a push button knob to play a certain game. I developed the concept of borrowing several T.V. game shows that had contestants pushing a knob or button to be the first to win a prize or contest. The creation of the box was first conceived in my mind. I've found that with leadership, many creative thoughts enter our spirits and minds. We, however, must have the boldness to pursue them and not 'short change ourselves' nor the Lord with doubts. If you can envision it, God can make it come to pass. And yes, the introduction and display of the Strong's Concordance, The New Bible Dictionary, The Bethany Parallel

Commentary, and The New Layman's Parallel Bible were all brought into the class to help explain and encourage all attendees to dive a little deeper into the word of God.

ARTICLES WRITTEN

During times of barrenness, suffering, or perhaps isolation, some individuals use the time productively. Instead of 'wasting time,' they put their time to good use. However, many may not see it that way. However, if a person finds him/herself incarcerated or alone for a long period of time, or goes through broken relationships, or battles cancer, those realities of life may in fact mold that person to become a prolific writer who then inspires many. We are told that our National Presider Emeritus used his 'voluntary vacation' to pen many of the articles and lessons we now study. During that time, he used the opportunity to gather his thoughts together and write. I suppose the lesson learned here is to be productive while the opportunity permits and not squander the time.

Back in the 1990s I found myself writing a number of articles as well as songs. It was a time when songs and articles 'flowed' constantly in me, through me, and from me. I effortlessly wrote songs and often was inspired to sit and write an article until it was completed. I also delved into writing my own gospel tracts, and used the format created by 'Chick Tracts.' The tracts that they put out were eye-catching because they used the simple format of a cartoon layout, and everyone likes to read a good cartoon. So, I adopted the format and created what I call my own "FlapTract." Gifted with a creative nature by the Lord, I was inspired to also create a public display stand which was placed in the Fellowship Hall at our main church (415 Atlantic Ave.). Brightly colored, the display stand was called, "From the Pacific End." Many of my tracts and articles were posted in the sleeves of the display stand, and each Sunday they were made available to the general membership.

Of the numerous articles that I wrote at that time, "Satan, the deceptive deceiver" was one of the longest that I have ever penned. Incredibly enough, it took me a year to complete it. It may have been due to the start/stop I was experiencing at the time, or the fact that 'life,' with its many demands kept me away from completing it within a certain amount of time. In the article, I wanted to expose Satan for what he is, and the many tactics he uses to ensnare the people of God. "Tarry Until" was another long piece that was written. Growing up Catholic, the Holy Ghost and tarrying were all new to me. I did not know at the time what it meant to be filled with the Holy Ghost, nor the process of tarrying for it. At that time, it all seemed foreign to me. However, experiencing the prayer service, and watching what happened when folks became filled with the Spirit taught me some valuable lessons. Thus, I attempted to put on paper my thoughts of what people needed to be aware of when tarrying for the Spirit of God. And the first heading that I started the article with, was 'Fear.' I started the article that way because growing up Catholic, and seeing folks shout, dance, and speak in tongues became a little too dramatic for me. I wanted to address it head-on and dispel the fear factor. Other writings included: "Why does God Allow?," "Get Real," "Christmas Questions," "But, the word that hinders," "What's Deadlier than Aids?," "In Response to 911 – a word to America/a word to the church," "May I Remind You," "In the Interim," "The Secret of Silence," "Psychic or Sidekick," "System Override," "And What about You?," "At Your Expense," "And Where is Daddy?" "You Can Make the Difference," "Smooth," "Why Jesus is better than Santa Claus," "Easter, let's keep it Real," "What Christmas Ain't," "What is Hype?.". and more. For those who wanted to engage in street evangelism, the "Harvester's Institute' was written back in 1990. In it, instructions were given to anyone who wanted to witness to those on the street, in their neighborhoods or in the subway system. In my tenure at the mission, I would like to think that I used the 'time' wisely and wrote.

I also remember keeping a journal of our Sunday services. Within it, records were kept of who attended the service that day, what scripture and theme I used, and my personal feeling of how I thought the service went. I thought it necessary at the time to document what went on during our services. That practice became essential because it chronicled what my feelings and thoughts were during that time. Our National Presider Emeritus Rev. Herbert Daughtry always said to us (the ministers), "write." He recognized the importance in doing so, and I've come to see the virtues in doing so in the early stages of my ministry. Now, because of my early writings, I get a chance to see where my thoughts were during a particular year in my ministry, and depending on the substance matter, what my thoughts were and how I felt about a particular matter.

From time to time after our services, we would go down to our main church on Atlantic Avenue to continue the fellowship and participate in the worship service there. Part of my training involved 'watching and learning' what was happening around me; who was doing what; what was happening on the balcony when the service was 'hot;' where the ushers were, and so on. I observed several things because that was the way I was taught. Two documents that came out of my observations were the 'Minister's Critique Form,' and 'Pulpit Protocol.'

The intent behind the 'Minister's Critique Form' was to help build confidence in our ministers as they presented the 'Word' on a given day. The goal was for all the ministers to meet on a given day, pick a scriptural topic from a basket and deliver a 5-minute sermonette on which they would be critiqued by their peers. It would have been a way for us to grade ourselves in love, sharpen our skills and to equip each other with some level of confidence should we have to speak internally or outside of our church. Unfortunately, though several attempts were made to start it, it did not get off the ground.

The "Pulpit Protocol" was another document created with the same purpose in mind. In my opinion, several of the ministers needed a 'guide' to instruct them on what to do when handling primarily the Sunday service. Under each section of the Order of Service of our main church, I took the liberty of breaking down what can happen when each section is done. With short phrases following a section, I gave examples to help minimize the anxiety that can happen when a person does not know exactly what to say to the congregation. Moreover, at the start of the 'Pulpit Protocol,' I purposely inserted the wording, "It is not a protocol that is 'written in stone,' however, one should first learn the basics of the protocol and once reaching a level of familiarity, deviate at their leisure." Again, it was an attempt to intervene and assist those who needed assistance.

To anyone reading this, your church more than likely has a different 'Order of Service' set up. However, some of the basic wording examples stated here and protocols can also be applied to what happens in your own sanctuary. Prayerfully, this should provide some assistance to you and in your ministry.

Minister Critique Form

NAME:_____

DATE:_____

	YES	NO	N/A
0. Speaker's Attire/Dress Code Appropriate			
1. Speaker adjusted the mike			
2. Protocol Acknowledgement Done			
3. Prayed			
4. Good Posture			
5. Did Speaker Seem Nervous			
6. Did Speaker Seem Energetic/Confident			
7. Good Reading/Eye Contact			
8. Good Voice Projection			
9. Monotone Voice			
10. Nasal Voice			
11. Good Pronunciation of Words			
12. Good Use of Hands			
13. Excessive Scratching of Head/Nose/Eye/Ear			
14. Good Eye Contact			
15. Good Use of Pulpit Area			
16. Too Much Repetition of Words/Phrase			
17. Did Message Fit the Title			
18. Did Speaker's Message Drift from the Read Scripture(s)			
19. Appropriate Life Example Used			
20. Was 'Story Telling' Affective			
21. Was Joke(s) Affective			
22. Good Reading Pace			
23. Did Speaker 'Connect' with Audience			
24. Was Message Thorough			
25. Was message too short/long			

Addendum

Are you aware of the usher, choir, pulpit assoc. balcony etc.?
Was the offering collected?
Who collected the offering?
Who is singing for the service?

Comments

_____
_____
_____

Min. R. Watkis 5/26/04

PULPIT PROTOCOL

With the congregation standing, the person in charge should be prepared to lead the congregation in their theme song.

FELLOWSHIP TIME

Note: It should be understood that this segment of the service plays a vital part of the ministry. It is a time when the congregation gets the opportunity to meet and greet each other.

The person in charge should have a short phrase prepared to share with the congregation as they fellowship together. Example: "God bless you," "you're blessed," "you're going to make it," "you've got the victory," etc.

Note - Long phrases have the tendency to 'hold' a person in one area too long. Plus it shortens the fellowship between congregation members.

Note - The person in charge should also be sensitive not to prolong the fellowship time. Charges can 'move the service' along by initiating a congregational song.

HYMN

It is always a good practice to learn the Sunday hymn before the Sunday service. The person in charge can contact the main office and inquire which hymn will be sung on the given Sunday. If uncertain about the hymn, the person in charge should ask for help in learning the hymn.

Note - Leaders can also recommend a hymn that he/she is familiar with and ask that the hymn be included in the Sunday morning worship.

Note – On the designated Sunday; If the congregation is having difficulty singing the morning hymn, the leader should 'wisely' shorten the hymn by moving the congregation to the last verse and end the selection.

Note – Congregation should be standing during the hymn.

Note – Again, the person in charge should <u>not</u> over-bear the congregation by singing too loud into the microphone.

ANNOUNCEMENTS

Prior to the announcements being given, the leader should locate the announcer before the announcement part is reached within the service. If the charge person does not see the announcer, the leader should ascertain who would be giving the announcement.

Note – An extended announcement previously made, should be relayed to the pastor before the announcement is made and it should be left to the discretion of the pastor whether it is made a second time.

Rationale – 1. Depending on the length of the service, too many announcements can put a 'damper' on the flow of the service.

2. Some announcements may be dated well into the future.

3. After a certain length of time (and announcements), most people only retain the last few minutes of what was said.

MINISTRY OF GIVING AND RECEIVING – GOD'S TITHES

The person in charge should direct all who are paying their tithes to form a line in the center of the sanctuary and call for the trustees. Charge person should then read a related scripture on tithing as members assemble themselves. Once lined up, a short prayer should be said.

Note – During this portion of the service, all walking/talking should cease.

Note – The following verses can be used:

First Fruit – Prov. 3:9-10, Num. 18:12, Deut. 26:1-2, Ne. 10:34-35

Tithes – Ge. 28:22, Lev. 27:30, II Cor. 31:5, De. 12:6, Mal. 3:10

MINISTRY OF GIVING & RECEIVING – GENERAL OFFERING

In general, the person in charge should direct the congregation to stand as they prepare themselves to bring forth their general offering. A brief praycr should be said before the walking begins.

ACKNOWLEDGEMENT OF VISITORS

As we come to this part of the service, the charge person and congregation are afforded the opportunity to formally meet and greet all first-time visitors. The following is what can be said during this part of the service: "At this time we would like to acknowledge all those who are here for the first time. We ask that you stand, give us your name, and any brief words that you would like to share with us at this time." Note - the leader should pan the audience from left to right throughout the sanctuary to see all who are standing up. Once everyone has been acknowledged, the charge person may say the following: "On behalf of the pastor and first lady of this church, the ministerial staff and congregation, we would like to officially welcome you into our service."

SELECTION

On the heels of the Acknowledgement of Visitors, the charge person may say the following: "And to show how much we appreciate your fellowship with us, we would like to ask the choir to come and render you a special selection of their choosing."

CALL TO SALVATION/MEMBERSHIP

Any pulpit designate should be ready to direct a person where to stand as they are coming forward for salvation or to join the church.

Note – The pulpit designate should have the microphone ready and should not allow any person to come up to the immediate pulpit area.

Note – If the preacher asks the congregation to come forth for prayer, pulpit designates should be ready to assist the preacher with the 'flow' of the congregation in the altar area.

COMMUNION/ANOINTING SERVICES

If the preacher asks the congregation to come forth for prayer or communion, pulpit designates should be ready to assist the preacher in whatever manner possible.

Note - During the anointing service (if the pulpit designate is assisting), the pulpit designate should 'gently usher' the congregant forward and *raise their hands to be prayed for so that the minister does not have to lean forward to 'reach for the people.'*Hands raised denotes a sign of surrender to the Lord.

written by: Min. R. Watkis – 8/99

SOME EXTERNAL APPROACHES TO MINISTRY

The African People Christian Organization (A.P.C.O.), was one of many organizations created by our National Presider Emeritus, Rev. Dr. Herbert Daughtry. What I believe its intent was, was to highlight the achievements and Afrocentricity of Christians not only in the pages of scriptures, but also in everyday life itself. From that, a broadcast was started on the radio station WWRL 1600 AM and brother Leroy Applin headed the segment. As time moved on, the broadcast was divided into four segments; one of which landed on my lap. As it is my nature then (and still now), I mixed the subject matter to make it more appealing to my listeners. One major obstacle I encountered that had to be addressed was fear. In this instance, the broadcast reminded me of our tarry service which was held at our main church. When it was time for the broadcast, I got nervous as the hour approached and found myself almost falling apart from the notion that hundreds (if not thousands) of people would be listening to me that day. Till one day, I stopped for a moment and found a way to encourage myself. I said, "So what if I make a mistake? Is someone going to come through the mike and choke me?" The other thing that gave me confidence is when I decided to 'be myself' and convey that over the airwaves. There was no need for me to be rigid to a certain format of broadcasting. I figured, if I liked myself, then others would too. When that was settled within me, the segments became a breeze to do. Ironically, when I had nervous guests on the broadcast, I found that my calm demeanor settled them also.

That mindset of being oneself should carry itself into your ministry also. One should not become a 'carbon copy' of someone else. Again, once I made the decision to be myself for the broadcast, peace came about. In fact, when the live broadcast started, I would say to people over the airwaves, "You can come down to the church by car, train, walking, bus or even jumping out of a plane." I decided to flip the whole thing around and joke with my listening audience. Be yourself and don't worry about imitating someone else. Be yourself because only you know you. Once you come to that realization, everything else will fall in line.

TRACT DISTRIBUTION ON NOSTRAND/FULTON STREETS

Part of our outreach ministry involved proselytizing in the Pacific Street area. From time to time, I would gather whoever was willing and we found ourselves on either Nostrand Avenue or on Fulton Street handing out tracts. Those two areas in the Restoration section of Brooklyn supplied an abundance of people for us to engage with. Many businesses, eateries and banks were found on Fulton Street. Nostrand Avenue had the same except for banks. Banking would be found further up the street. In our outreach in the community, I did not use the standard 'tract' that many churches used. We used our own. As I've stated before, I borrowed the concept from "Chick Tract" and created a folded two-panel or an eight-panel tract. In addition, the tract had to be 'relevant and direct' without much reading and legible enough with the proper font size and spacing. Through the years, I accepted tracts from other church folks that I really did not care for. The overall message was there, but (in my opinion), it got swallowed up by the design, arrangement, and wordiness of the reading. So, I used the comic book format, because I found that people would rather read a short comic strip with pictures, than a tract that is too wordy and lengthy.

Another concept that I had in mind was to use 'headings' that were either provocative or controversial to the reader. For instance, one tract was entitled, "And Where is Daddy?" Another was, "You Can Make the Difference." The first tract's intent was to call attention to the fact that many of our 'fathers' were missing in the lives of their children. Their sperm reached the egg, but nine months after that, many were nowhere to be found. So, we had many youngsters growing up without their biological fathers. With the other, "You Can Make the Difference," I purposely used an image of Dr. Martin Luther King to hopefully grab the attention of my readers. Within the content of the tract, I attempted to make an appeal to the reader that she/he could be the catalyst to bring about change; to make a difference. However, one tract that I wrote, I knew it was going to bring on a negative response from people just seeing the heading. The tract was entitled, "Is Your Child Stupid?" As offensive as the title was, I stuck with it anyway. When distributed, the frowns that I got from those who received it were enough to kill. However, the approach that I took with that tract was not to lift whether our children were stupid or not, but instead to focus the attention on us as adults who constantly do stupid things in the presence of our children. Any parent would speak highly of the intelligence of their child. You would always hear phrases such as, "She started walking before she turned two," or "I heard him say 'da-da' when he was just 14 months old." So, the attempt was to dramatize to the adults that our children's minds are brilliant. Therefore, we as adults should not put damaging examples of wording and behavior before our children because our kids are learning what they see and hear from us.

So, with some tenacity, I created, and we distributed, the tracts in those two locations in Brooklyn because we wanted to reach as many people as possible. We also displayed on the back of our tracts all of the information needed for anyone who was interested in visiting our mission.

CHRISTMAS CAROLING

Believe it or not, we did attempt on one occasion to go door to door singing Christmas songs during the winter season; an action which I have never seen anyone in the black community do. This was another attempt to reach our neighbors to let them know that we were in the community. From the few homes where we stopped, the reception was cordial. I really don't remember who suggested we do that, or where the idea came from. It may have been done under the leadership of the previous pastor, Roger Howell, but the fact was, we did it! We went outside of the box of being "Churchie" and provided a service to the community that was different. I think by us doing that, it challenged all to go outside of their comfort zone to do something they had never done before, and secondly, the community witnessed something that they ordinarily don't see; Christians singing Christmas carols.

CHRISTMAS GIFT SOCKS

Still, within the Christmas season, the idea of giving out gifts to some of the neighbors on the block took root in our minds, and before long, a process developed to do just that. Several members from our main church at 415 Atlantic Avenue came over to give me a hand with that project. Of the memberships there were: Deacon Betty Brazell, Sister Darlene Bryant, Deacon Pam Williams, Sister Elease Watson, and three little helpers, Ayinde Watson, Joy & Carlos Jesse Jr. Everyone rolled up

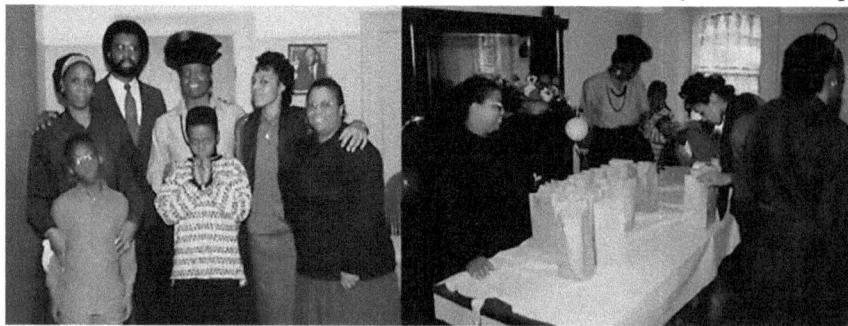

their sleeves and went to work. They all volunteered with a Godly spirit of encouragement and support, an act that will last with me for years to come. With some of the funds that were available, we purchased toothpaste, toothbrushes, soap, deodorant, hair combs, brushes, and Afro picks. Back then some of the items were also donated by my former employer Coler Memorial Hospital. All items were neatly bagged in our Fellowship Room and then notices were given to an apartment building on the following block from the mission. However, as with prior announcements made, folks from the apartment building still did not come out to receive what we had prepared for them. (So) Undeterred, I found myself going from door to door reminding people that the mission had gifts that were waiting to be given out. Slowly, one by one of our neighbors came out to receive the blessing we had prepared for them.

THANKSGIVING BLESSINGS

Like the Christmas Gift Sock giveaway, we did the same thing during one of the Thanksgiving seasons. However, this time a bit more creative work went into securing what we needed to provide for the community. In retrospect, I never held to the belief that the body of Christ should be a 'confined entity unto itself.' But that in the course of life, it should

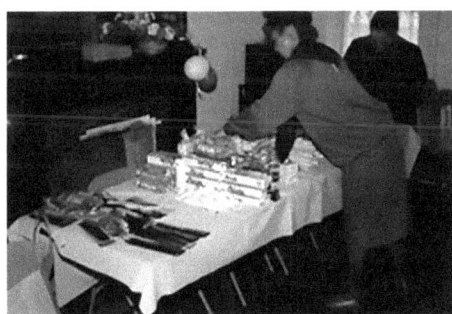 lead the way in all aspects of life; ultimately pointing to the way of Christ by example and action.

Instead of going into our treasury to buy stuff, we took a different approach. There is a word called, 'reciprocate' that comes to mind when thinking about what we did back in the day. The thought was, since many of the businesses on Fulton Street were frequented by black folks, owners of these businesses should reciprocate and supply us with what we needed. After all, 'fair is fair'…amen? So, we went to the local merchants with a stamped letter from our main church and asked each merchant to help and assist us with some of their non-perishable items so that we could be a blessing to those in the community who did not have Thanksgiving. All of them did, except one. Despite showing a bona fide stamped letter of our intentions, this merchant did not comply with our request. So, a more stringent approach was employed. I had asked some of the brothers to come with me as we re-visited that same store. It was not long before we received full cooperation from that store.

In addition to that, two other methods were used to accomplish our goal of blessing the community. One was the help of some of the sisters from our main church (415), and the other was the place where I worked at the time; Coler Memorial Hospital. With the renovation of our kitchen area and a functioning stove, some of the sisters came over and started preparing the Thanksgiving meal. Some of them, like Minister Dorothy Isaac and her sister Deacon Rosa Potts even started the preparation from their homes. Thank God for our sisters. These sisters came again, with a willing heart and a helpful attitude to get the job done.

The method I had used at Coler Memorial Hospital was a more 'direct' one. I simply went to the administrators and said, "I need some money from you because we are trying to feed the homeless during the Thanksgiving season." Without hesitation, all of them complied. However, let me say here that there is something to be said when a person has a good "rep." The reason I state that is because, when you have a good reputation, it goes far and takes you far in life. Because I had garnered a good reputation on the job site, there was no need for me to go into any explanation of what I was doing, or whether they could trust me or not. They simply gave, and I thank God for that.

The targeted area in the neighborhood was the Armory on Bedford Avenue. Like other Armories in the Brooklyn area, it provided sustenance and/or shelter to some of the misfortunates who did not have employment or families to resort to. There, I was able to contact a 'point person' in the Armory and the time and date was set for the food distribution. However, when the time and date came, the recipients were nowhere to be found. Part of our Sisterhood had prepared the victuals in our kitchen and from their homes. But folks were not there. So, I found myself going to and entering the Armory only to find several brothers sitting in what seemed like a gymnasium watching a 19-inch television. Without hesitation I went up to the stage where the television was and turned it off. I then announced who I was and verbally gave an open invitation to all who wanted to come with me to the mission to receive a plate of food. Some of the brothers came and were blessed by the marvelous food we had prepared for them. That venture of feeding the homeless was also repeated during the Christmas season.

MINISTERING AT THE SENIOR CITIZEN NURSING HOME

I don't recall how it happened, or what year it was, but part of our 'outreach' ministry led us to a Nursing Home in the mission area. As I have stated before, I did not believe in being a silent entity in the community. I guess I took my lead from what happened on the day of Pentecost. What that lesson highlighted for me was that God chose the most opportune time to 'show Himself.' In other words, the day of Pentecost did not happen in a vacuum, but at a moment when 'the stage was right, and all the characters were in place.' My point here is that we were in the community and needed to make a difference and needed to be seen. So, we went out, out into a new area of ministry. Out into a new environment. Out into and among a new challenge in ministry; ministering to our seniors. From one extreme to another, the question that is asked is, "How do you minister Christ to someone who probably knew Him longer and had a personal relationship with Him before you did?" The other extreme question might be, "How do you speak of Christ to a 4th grader?" To someone else, these questions might seem easy, but in my opinion, they require a bit of wisdom when ministering. After all, the Word does say, "The fruit of the righteous *is* a tree of life; and he that winneth souls *is* wise" (Pro 11:30). Even though the venture with our seniors did not last long, it was a 'hopeful' experience.

DOOR TO DOOR VISITS

The traditional door to door visits were done periodically while there at the mission. We wanted to know the neighborhood and wanted the neighborhood to know us. Along with writing my own tracts, it also gave me the 'boldness' to engage with people I did not know. I also started developing the technique of 'listening' to people and what they said to what they did not say. Looking at them while they spoke and taking notice of their 'body language' gave me much insight in witnessing people. Those who shared their time responded differently from those who were in a rush or did not want to listen. I also learned not to get offended when I was rejected by someone. The experience also provided a time to investigate the 'wisdom' of going out in pairs; more specifically, a male and a female, when possible. I found that it wards off any potential snares should the person who is being witnessed decides to flirt or attempt to 'guide' the conversation in a different direction. If that should arise, the other witnessing partner can step in to redirect the focus back to the church and Christ. In our visitations we were able to introduce ourselves and the mission to the neighborhood and not confine ourselves solely indoors. Again, I thank God for those willing souls who came out with me to engage in this vital part of ministry.

F.O.V.A.V.

F.O.V.A.V. is the acronym for the organization "Families of Victims Against Violence." It was an organization developed by our National Presider Emeritus Rev. Dr. Herbert D. Daughtry. Moved by families who were experiencing violent senseless death (primarily by police officers) and street crimes, Pastor Daughtry formed the group to provide an avenue of comfort and support to people who had experienced such tragedies. Sister Pat Middleton (deceased) was the chairperson of the group with sister Amy Council as the group's vice chair. A chaplain for the group was needed and I was asked to fill that position. In our meeting time, each member had the opportunity to share their experiences with each other. Some of the accounts shared were very heart moving and disturbing. To hear of a young life ending in a graphic violent way tugged at the heartstring of every one's soul in the Fellowship Room. And naturally, the tears followed. So, as the chaplain of the group, I was constantly challenged with ways of providing healing, an open ear and prayerfully a way to encourage a loved one, a parent or a grandmother with words of comfort. Those experiences were not easy. I had to find a way to bury my own emotions while showing 'hope' to those who were suffering.

From time to time the group met in the Fellowship Hall at our main church on Atlantic Ave. Soon after, the group held its first anniversary where other family members came out to acknowledge and support their family member who had died. I remember one of the ways the group connected with each other was through a quilt which was made with pieces of material donated from each member within the group. It was proudly displayed at subsequent anniversaries held at our main church. After several years of remembrance, the time came when I felt that the group needed to shift their attention from 'mourning' to 'laughter.' In other words, rather than meeting and rehearsing events of a loved one that moved everyone to tears, I thought it would be more beneficial if the group recounted a funny or hilarious moment they had with their family member before his/her passing. In my opinion, it would have served a more therapeutic moment to have the membership and those in attendance laughing, rather than crying.

Unfortunately, before the idea could get off the ground, sickness touched the life of the chairperson Sister Pat Middleton, and she passed shortly after. I had also shared the concept with Sister Amy, but the group had reached a low attendance level and the thought just fizzled away. Till this day, I would have liked to see what would have happened if F.O.V.A.V had taken a different approach to their gatherings and anniversaries.

BOWERY MISSIONS (FEMALE & MEN)

Sr. Min. Alice B. Edwards was introduced to the Bowery Mission for Women in lower Manhattan by one of the sisters of our main church on Atlantic Avenue, sister Elnora. The Mission was attended by women who were attempting to stabilize their lives from destructive habits and behaviors. During the week, Min. Edwards would go down to the mission to minister and encourage the women there. I don't know the precise length of time that she engaged the women, but the time came when I was asked to continue the visits in her place. The change may have been due to the location of the mission, or the fact that I drove, and she didn't. I accepted the challenge and went. Under the leadership of our Presider Emeritus Herbert Daughtry, I had gained some experience in ministering to an incarcerated female population and was aware and told of the possibility of 'assimilation.' In other words, I had to be mindful that some of the women under those conditions may use the opportunity to win the attraction of a gullible person for whatever their intent may have been. Therefore, in attending the Bowery Mission for Women, I had positioned myself to be cautious when speaking, looking, or even holding hands in prayer.

The women were receptive to the call of the Bible study sessions, which usually lasted approximately one hour. It gave me a chance to listen to their stories and share the Word of God with them. The number of attendees ranged from 4 to 5 women and the age difference varied. Even though they attended the sessions, I could tell that not everyone really appreciated the hour. Some came because it was a requirement of the mission that they attend.

I found the experience very rewarding because it took me into a different part of the 'vineyard' and I was exposed to a segment of God's creation that had come under difficult situations in life. They were not the regular 'churchy' folks we see every Sunday at church. They did not go around saying, "Praise the Lord" to each other. Their realities were different. Some sold their bodies while others had drugs running through their veins. Now the challenge that I faced was, "What can I say to these women to encourage them and give them a sense of hope? What can I say to them to remind them that they are still precious in the sight of God?" Ahh, therein lies the difference and the challenge for us as 'Christians;' for isn't it easier to carry our Bibles in our hands as we wave to each other or greet one another with a 'holy kiss and hug?' Isn't it easier to dress up on a Sunday morning, get inside our cars or even board the transit system and arrive at our church to 'praise God' with a shout and a dance? However, the challenge comes when we read scripture such as, "Then saith He unto his disciples, The harvest truly *is* plenteous, but the labourers *are* few" (Mat 9:37), or, Luke 10:30-37 "And Jesus answering said, A certain *man* went down from Jerusalem to Jericho, and fell among thieves, which stripped him of his raiment, and wounded *him,* and departed, leaving *him* half dead. And by chance there came down a certain priest that way: and when he saw him, he passed by on the other side. And likewise, a Levite, when he was at the place, came and looked at him, and passed by on the other side. But a certain Samaritan, as he journeyed, came where he was: and when he saw him, he had compassion *on him,* and went to *him,* and bound up his wounds, pouring in oil and wine, and set him on his own beast, and brought him to an inn, and took care of him. And on the morrow when he departed, he took out two pence, and gave *them* to the host, and said unto him, take care of him; and whatsoever thou spendest more, when I come again, I will repay thee. Which now of these three, thinkest thou, was neighbour unto him that fell among the thieves? And he said, "He that shewed mercy on him." Then said Jesus unto him, "Go, and do thou likewise."

When other areas of the vineyard are presented to us, it brings with it a sense of unfamiliarity, doesn't it? We find ourselves a bit nervous trying to navigate through areas we are not familiar or comfortable with. But isn't that what ministry is supposed to be? It reminds me again of the time I went inside the Armory on Bedford Avenue in Brooklyn and turned off a television that several brothers were watching at the time.

Ministry at the Bowery Mission for Women went on for several months and then an opportunity was opened for me to switch over to the Bowery Mission for Men.

The Bowery Mission for Men was altogether a different challenge. These were men who were out on the street under additional conditions. They were homeless, family-less, drug addicted, jobless, mentally challenged and 'busted.' So again, the challenge was, how do you minister to people in those conditions? How do you present Christ to a person who comes to the mission for a meal and who doesn't have a permanent residence he can call 'home?' The approach that I took at that time was to address them as 'men.' Brother James Macklin, who was the Acting Director at the time, introduced me to the brothers. The large room where the brothers assembled resembled a large sanctuary with many pews. I remember being introduced, and they made a conscious decision that I was not going to 'coddle' them in any way. I did not want to be insensitive to their struggles in life, but neither did I want to present the usual passivity that some preachers preached. A 'pie-in-the-sky' presentation of the gospel was not on the agenda for a preached word to those brothers. Instead, I dealt with them as 'men.' Through my own examples and a couple of jokes thrown in, I was able to capture the attention of some of the brothers in the room. I dealt with them as 'men,' and not as some persons to be 'pitied.' The experiences at the mission gave me new insights to another part of what ministry is about. In other words, I was outside the proverbial box dealing with a segment of God's people, and it felt great!

In my visits, one brother from our main church said to me one day that he would like to come with me to the Bowery Men's Mission. There were others who made the trip to the mission with me, but this one brother stood out. His name was James McCornell. He later became a precious friend and brother to me. I suppose he stood out because others accepted the offer to come, while he 'requested.' In our conversations, he shared with me that he wanted to engage in that ministry because he needed something more than just going to church on a Sunday. When he came, he came prepared and ready to engage with the brothers in the service. I took note of that! Most people are not inclined and are quite hesitant to engage themselves with the homeless population. They are not as willing to fling their hands up to say, "Here I am, send me." But James did. I will forever remember that. I will also remember one comical moment when James and I went to the mission, and as usual, the mission offered us some pastries to take. From time to time, eating places would donate the leftovers to the mission for those who came to grab a bite to eat. Well, in their surplus, the Bowery offered us a couple of boxes of pastries as we returned to the main church on Atlantic Avenue. When we arrived, I grabbed the boxes to share with those inside of the church, however, James swiftly said, "Brother Minister, what are you doing?." So, I told him that I was going to share the coffee cakes and muffins with those inside of the church. He abruptly stated, "Yeah, but those "n******" didn't come with us!" That jovial moment, as often as I think about it, will forever bring me laughter, and forever be sketched in my mind.

MINISTERED WITH PASTOR HERBERT DAUGHTRY AT A PENAL INSTITUTION

As I have just mentioned in my visits to the Bowery Mission for Females, there was also a time when some of the congregation went with the Presider, Rev. Dr. Herbert Daughtry to one of the penal systems in Manhattan. It was my first experience ministering to that population and I soon learned that one must be mindful that some people behind bars may in fact use their 'charm' and what seems 'interest' to gain a willing victim's attention. In other words, if not careful, a person may find himself succumbing to the enticement of a person who has lost a great level of freedom and may be looking for a gullible person to either run errands or emotionally get trapped up with them. One occasion, one of the sisters from our main church on Atlantic Avenue pulled my 'coattail' and told me to be careful of that entrapment.

Being members of The House of the Lord Church, we were exposed through Rev. Dr. Daughtry to different aspects of ministry. There were times we found ourselves on our knees at the altar, and other times marching across the Manhattan Bridge in protest. There was no dichotomy between church and state. The gospel, as presented in the Holy text, sees no separation between engaging in the social while laying one's alms at the altar. In my opinion, therein lies the difference between our doctrine and others. I always found it interesting how some Christians, when in trouble with law enforcement or in need of political assistance, resorted to seeking out our church. While at the same time, their pastor, their leadership, preached separation of church and state. It reminded me of the time we went to Buffalo NY to support Author

Eve in his race for mayor. We marched down the streets of Buffalo and came across a certain church. Some of its members were standing inside the gate that separated the sidewalk from the church building. When we tried to get their support in supporting candidate Eve, their response was, "we don't get involved in politics." That response however comes in distinct contrast to the gospel of Christ. For instance, on the onset of his ministry, the scroll was handed to Jesus to read, and the Bible stated that he found the place which read, "The Spirit of the Lord *is* upon me, because he hath anointed me to preach the gospel to the poor; he hath sent me to heal the brokenhearted, to preach deliverance to the captives, and recovering of sight to the blind, to set at liberty them that are bruised, To preach the acceptable year of the Lord"- Lu. 4:18-19. If that scriptural reference wasn't a political statement, I don't know what is.

TRACT DISTRIBUTION WITH THE BIBLE STUDY GROUP

As I also reflected on some of the ventures we've engaged in, there were times when the program was altered to 'mix it up' a bit. I conducted Bible studies in several locations; one of which was in our main church on Atlantic Ave. Someone once said, "familiarity breeds contempt," so on one occasion, I decided to take the Bible study group outside on the street to distribute some tracts. My nature is not one that sticks to one thing and 'rides it out' until eternity. From time to time, I like to change up or as I've just stated, 'mix it up' to hopefully interject a bit of freshness in whatever we are doing. That's just the way I am. It kind of reminds me of the scripture where it states, "Behold, I will do a new thing; now it shall spring forth; shall ye not know it? I will even make a way in the wilderness, *and* rivers in the desert." (Isa 43:19)

Believing that they had come out to continue with their study, the Bible study group quickly learned they were going out to distribute tracts in the Downtown area of Brooklyn. Now, one main difference was that we didn't use the standard tracts that many churches used, but we used our own; more specifically, the ones I created. As I've said before, I just did not like the tracts that other churches were using. In my opinion, there was no appeal to the pamphlet. Just a lot of words. I'm sure the content was scriptural, but there just wasn't any attraction to the tracts. And, in my study of marketing strategies, there was no 'hook' to the literature; nothing for the reader to say, "Oh yeah, let me read this." Just a lot of words. So, we went out with some of my own. I used the one with the image of Dr. Martin Luther King on it entitled, "You Can Make the Difference." The first thing that stood out about that tract was the image of Dr. King speaking to the masses. Secondly, the heading, "You Can Make the Difference" was again a statement to tie the reader into the content of the tract; "What difference can I make?" Thirdly, the image on the tract was that of a Black man. It was something identifiable, not an image of a European with long straight hair and blue eyes sitting on a rock caressing a lamb. The people who received the tract in the Downtown area, could relate to the image that they saw on the tract. So, I mixed it up and we were able to not only study the Word of God, but to also take the gospel out on the street.

PERFORMED SEVERAL WEDDINGS

In my tenure at the Pacific Street mission, I was asked to perform several weddings. Though it was my honor to participate, I need to highlight several things and put in perspective how I was able to perform the task of carrying through with the ceremony. I think upon my elevation in ministry, The Broadman Minister's Manual, a small handbook, was given to me and became the guide in helping me to accomplish various ceremonial tasks. In it, there are several not only verses one can use, but also instructions on how a ceremony may be performed. It is a valuable tool. It was also important for me to be recognized by the New York City State as a bona fide Minister of the Gospel of Jesus Christ. To accomplish this, I went downtown Manhattan to City Hall with certain documents to certify me as a minister. Therefore, I was able to perform weddings. Some of the documents that I took with me included, the HOLC incorporation papers, a letter of recommendation and proof of residency. Though I had not received any formal training in performing a wedding, I had to 'muster up enough confidence and wing it' before those in attendance at the ceremony. Again, this is where the 'Broadman Minister's Manual' came in handy. In addition to using the book as a guide, I intentionally interjected my own thoughts on what the relationship of marriage ought to be. Examples of our ancestors were included; the design of God for man and woman was included; the sanctity of the marriage bond was also included. I found myself speaking on these topics not only to the two people standing in front of me, but to the audience as well. They, too, needed to be reminded.

Not too long after I had performed several ceremonies, the thought came into my mind that our ministers also needed to be trained in these areas: how do you perform a wedding, baptism, christening, funeral etc. It was a bit nerve racking for me trying to 'wing-it,' but it should not be so for our ministers who were coming up the rank of ministry. I therefore took additional steps in creating a system where our ministers could be trained in several aspects of the ministry as well as in certain protocols. The steps included:

PROPER PROTOCOLS – (The intent) to train the ministers to acknowledge officers, pastors, bishop(s) when called to the pulpit area.

PULPIT CRITIQUE – (The intent) a form created several years ago that can be used to critique each minister as they present a message/sermonette to their peers.

SPONTANEOUS SPEAKING/PREACHING – (The intent) this can be a spontaneous time when each minister can receive a familiar scripture to speak on for 5 minutes. The process can be filmed for critique purposes. It can also be used to teach each minister how to draw on what they've already learned from the scriptural text to create their sermon.

WRITING SCENARIOS - (The intent) a 15/20-minute time frame where the ministers can be given a brief problem-solving scenario to see how they address difficulties that may arise. Also, the time can be used in writing a 'child story' for the young. This may show how imaginary and creative the minister can be.

PERSONAL TESTIMONY – (The intent) a time to hear from the individual minister about what they are doing, and hopefully provide some assistance, encouragement and direction to help them in their various ventures.

PULPIT ANTICIPATION – (being aware of what's happening in the service. Example: having water for the minister when he/she coughs or constantly clears their throats, untangling the mike cord when tangled, directing reader and people to the podium to speak or read.

PROCESSIONAL ORDER – (The intent) the line-up of the leadership when it comes to processing out of the chapel, processing during the communion, processing during the convocation.

PEOPLE COMING STRAIGHT TO THE PULPIT – (The intent) as mentioned, minister in the pulpit or on the front pew directing visitors to use the podium and not come directly to the pulpit.

HARVESTER'S INSTITUTE
Material written and compiled by: Min. R. Watkis, 9/29/1990

Purpose/Goal: To instruct and prepare the Christian in effective street evangelism and witnessing techniques.

1. Pray before going out

2. Overcome personal handicap(s) – fear, shyness, etc.

3. Carry only what you need

4. Go out in pairs – (ideal, male/female....one witness, the other prays)

5. Know your material – also where to find particular scriptures

6. Posture, hygiene and appearance is important

7. Show interest – if possible, you may want to shake a person's hand

8. Go where the people are

9. Don't argue or preach people to hell

10. Do not resent people for not showing interest or throwing tracks away

11. If you don't have an answer, get their name and phone # and get back to the person. DO NOT GIVE OUT PERSONAL PHONE NUMBERS, RATHER GIVE THE CHURCH' PHONE NUMBER FOR CONTACT.

12. Be sensitive when to continue and/or move on

13. Encountering a different ideology, persuasion or faith; we're not there to argue or fight.

14. Final objective is to provide the knowledge of Salvation.

TECHNIQUES

Always access your environment & people to determine what technique to use. Example: witnessing to a youth may be different from witnessing to a mother. You may grab the youth's attention when sharing a sporting event than recipes for cooking. Likewise, the same can be said for an older adult.

APPROACHES

The following statements may be used:

"God bless you brother/sister"

"Here's little something for you to read"

"Have a blessed day"

"God bless you brother/sister, can I have 2 minutes of your time"

"Excuse me brother/sister, have you heard the good news?"

"God bless you brother/sister, can I share some important news with you?"

"Yo, what's up?"

As time went on, it became gratifying seeing several forums, workshops and opportunities put in place to provide training to our ministers.

DISTRICT FELLOWSHIP WITH THE N.E. CHURCHES

I believe I gave testimony earlier about the creation of our church's outdoor sign. If you'd recall, I spoke about a truck carrying steel sheets that broke off the truck and I rolled up one of the sheets and put it in the back of my Hyundai, and how that sheet became our church outside sign. Well, I lift that up again because the name that was painted on the sign was, "The House of the Lord Fellowship Center." The concept of 'fellowship' was riding high in my spirit, and I wanted to engage more in it. The time came when a number of changes were made by the National Presider and the Board of Elders, and I was elevated from the position of Pioneer Minister to the position of Northeast District Minister. However, what I felt then while ministering as the assigned leader of the Pacific Street Mission, I felt the same in my new title. I felt that it was not enough for our churches to only meet 3 or perhaps 4 times a year for an annual event; the fellowship needed to continue. So, throughout the year, arrangements were made for the Pacific Street Mission to begin a fellowship with our church in the city of Philadelphia. At that time my tenure as Pioneer Minister had come to an end and Sr. Min. Dorothy Isaac became the minister in charge at the Pacific Street Mission. Our first attempt to engage in fellowship took place, but due to the length of time in traveling from Brooklyn NY to Philadelphia PA, some of the membership from the Philadelphia church could not wait and went home. However, we did meet and started the process. Now in the position as the Northeast District Minister, I wanted to increase the fellowship process within the district. With my new assignment, I was able to unite in fellowship some of the brothers from our main church on Atlantic Avenue with the Jamaica Queens Church. Some of the brothers from the Atlantic Avenue congregation also went with me to Philadelphia and from Philadelphia, plans were in the works to stop next in Bergen County, New Jersey to fellowship with Evangelist Dawn Daughtry and her congregation. As I've mentioned before, the fellowship in the district needed to be expanded so that folks in the south could greet and meet those from the north. Pastors in the northeast could then share with each other ideas, achievements and challenges they encountered in an atmosphere of leisure and fellowship. Plus, it needed to be ongoing, not just twice or three times per year. Not only would the fellowship be beneficial to the pastors, but to the congregation as well. In addition, rather than just hearing a name without a face, the fellowship would remedy that. People would know who brother or sister "so and so" is and was.

SOME OF THE CREATIVE OUTREACH ATTEMPTS ROOFTOP BELLS

For a minute, I became 'Catholic;' let me explain. I took notice of the bells that were rung during the week from some Catholic churches in Brooklyn. So, the thought came to my mind, "Why not attempt the same thing?" In other words, why not ring bells on a Sunday morning to announce to the community that we are beginning our service? So, with the creativity that the Lord has blessed me with, I placed a speaker in the front window of the mission and played bell sounds with the keyboard I had at the time. Feeling that it wasn't reaching far enough, I then placed the speaker on the roof of the building. It may have looked crazy, but I was searching for a creative way to reach the community. I even went as far as putting out flyers reminding the community to "listen for the bells." Well, that venture did not last too long. After a short period, and a bit of inclement weather, the large speaker came down.

COFFEE HOUSE

The concept of a 'Coffee House' originated under the leadership of Pastor Roger Howell. We met indoors and ate 'crumpets' with tea or coffee. However, after Pastor Howell left, I decided to continue with the concept. But instead of having it indoors where no one could see or join us, we went outdoors. During the winter months, the coffee urn along with instant coffee, tea bags, sugar, stirrers, coffee cakes, biscuits, chairs, a table and balloons were placed in front of the mission. And every and anyone passing by was invited to freely partake of what we had on the table. It never made sense to me to 'be a church and hide in a corner.' Some did stop by and helped themselves to what we offered. That creative venture went on for a 'minute,' but sadly to say, it did not yield the outcome that I had expected. So it ended.

YOUTH SUNDAY SCHOOL

In time, we befriended some of the youth on the block. Some of them eventually attended our Sunday service and the idea of creating a Sunday School was born. However, I was always cautious of having kids in the building without an adult member of their family. I will soon speak about that in our next heading. Looking for assistance and someone who would involve themselves in teaching our Sunday School, I asked Sister 'Angie' (Angela Jones) to assume the responsibility of having some classes with the youth. Sister 'Angie' was one of the members of F.O.V.A.V. (Families of Victims Against Violence). She consented, and we proceeded. I think what kept the kids returning to the sessions were the free snacks they received after each class. From children to adults, food has always had a way of capturing the patience and time of people.

It may have started in the Sunday school where we made some attempts to teach the youth how to stand and speak in front of an audience. I understand that not everyone is comfortable speaking in front of a live audience. Having eyes on you, and people listening to the words that you are saying can be a bit unnerving. We believed that teaching the youth how to stand with confidence and articulate themselves was a plus for everyone. I remember some years later that City Councilman Charles Barron gave the same lessons to some of the brothers at our main church on Atlantic Avenue. I was in attendance, and as he taught us, I reflected on the teachings with the youth.

COMPUTER FUNDAMENTAL CLASS

In retrospect, I am amazed by some of the things that I've engaged in and the 'dares' I'd assumed. This brings to mind our Computer Fundamental Class. But before I go into that subject, let me share an experience I had with my older brother Orlando. One day, my brother Orlando and I found ourselves at the drive-thru windows of a K.F.C.

in Brooklyn. While there, I had placed an order and the attendant said that my order would take about five minutes before it would be ready. Jokingly I said, "Well, I should get something free if I have to wait." The attendant then said to me, "Okay, What do you want?" My reply to her question was, "How about a wing and a biscuit?" After she left to get my free wing and biscuit, my brother then turned and said to me, "See, that's your problem, you shouldn't have asked her for a wing and a biscuit, but a bucket!" The motto here is, "Don't short-change yourself (and the Lord) by thinking small." It is a lesson I now wish I had learned when an opportunity was opened up to me to acquire computers from the city.

One day I confronted the Executive Director at Coler Memorial Hospital. I had noticed during a particular year that the hospital was discarding several items that were still usable. However, the catch was, the staff could not take any items for themselves, because according to some city ordinances, the items had to be demolished and/or discarded. In addition, on some of the units in the institution, items such as beds, Hoyer lifters, new unopened cases of index cards, new three-ring binders, and small medication refrigerators, all had to be discarded. So, since one of the areas that was being renovated was my unit, I had 'cornered' the director of the hospital and inquired from him whether I could have some of the items that were slated for removal. He then said to me that he could not give me the okay, but that I should write a letter to H.H.C. (Health and Hospital Corporation) and put in my request. So, I did! It wasn't long after that that I received a call from H.H.C. informing me that a department in the lower part of Manhattan was shut down, and if I wanted, I could go down and see what I could use. In a matter of minutes, I placed a call to our main church on Atlantic Ave. and got a flatbed truck along with some brothers and we made our way to lower Manhattan.

When we arrived at the location, we entered a room where many computers, printer desks, metal and wooden file cabinets, carpet squares and chairs were made available to us. In my selection of what to take and leave, I made a horrible decision which still haunts me till this day. As a matter of fact, it brings back to mind the story I told about my brother while we waited at the K.F.C. pick-up window. Some of the items I saw in the room looked as if they had gone through the 'mill,' thus I decided not to take them, while others looked 'cleaner' than the rest. Brother James Simmons was one of the brothers who came with me, and I am very glad that he did. He 'overruled' one of my decisions to leave an old Xerox copy machine. In my mind, the machine looked old and dilapidated, but he saw something different. So, we took it. That old, dilapidated copy machine that I wanted to leave back, once fixed, was able to print out hundreds, if not thousands of materials that were used within the church. Thank God for his foresight! From our haul, we were able to secure computers, printers, carpet squares, chairs, a desk etc. from the closed office. As I have stated I made a horrible mistake by 'pickin-n-choosin' what to take from what not to take. The lesson here is, 'TAKE EVERYTHING!' Then once you have everything at your disposal, you can then 'pick and choose' what goes and what stays. In retrospect, we should have cleaned out that office and transported everything back to the mission where in my own time I could have taken the liberty to be more selective.

At the time we secured some of the items from the closed office, computers were not as prevalent as they are now. So, I decided to create what I called a "Computer Fundamental Class" at the mission. The goal was to introduce and educate some of the youth in the area about this technology. Again, computers were not as prevalent at that time, but the little that I knew about computers, I decided to put it to work. After deciding which machines to use, I organized about six computers to use for our class. The machines had to be cleaned physically and the hard drives had to be formatted and functional. Once set up, flyers were created, and the appeal was sent throughout the community that The House of the Lord Fellowship Center was offering computer classes to the community. The one stipulation that was put on the flyer was that $1.00 was asked by all participants when they came to the class. I remember the reaction of one adult woman when she read the flyer; she thought it was a hoax. I guess in her mind she probably thought, "No one gives a computer class for just $1.00." I should also state here that I again invoked the talents of my good friend James McCornell who was a retired electrician (at the time). James came in and ran all the wiring needed to conduct our classes. Each machine had its own power source. That brother saved me hundreds of dollars for the work that he did. Shortly after that, our Computer Fundamental Class was up and running. Kids came from different sections of the neighborhood, and I was able to teach them the 'basics' of the computer: what is a mouse and how to use it, what is the function of a keyboard, what is a monitor etc. They also learned how to make different shapes while watching the computer screen. I was also mindful to let the parents of the kids know where their children were, and what we were doing in the building. We also were very honored to have some of the brothers from our main church attend the class. Brothers Eugene Kirkland and Deacon. Joseph Horton were two of the participants. My two sons, Andwele and Ayinde

also attended. Back in my earlier years at Coler Memorial Hospital, I was introduced to this technology by Alex Batke, a Russian co-worker. He ran a brief class on the site using a Commodore 64 computer. From that time, I knew it was going to be something that would confront all of us. Technology was on its way, and we had to get ready for it. I also knew it was something that my two sons had to learn; therefore, I made every attempt to secure a system for the house. Back then I also felt that our churches needed to get ready for it, and so our Computer Fundamental Class was 'born.'

YOUTH CHOIR

With the steady presence of the youth on the block attending our computer classes, the thought came to mind, "Why not start a youth choir?" And so, I did. I have always been musically involved with several instruments as well as creating, singing, orchestrating, writing, and playing my own songs. So, with that in mind, I started the choir. My experience with several of the church groups such as: The House of the Lord Choir, The Gospel Chorus, The House of the Lord Mass Choir, playing my bass with Mark Turner and a group that Roger Howell and I started called Dedication, gave me the experience to handle the choir.

The group started, and we did our rehearsing inside the sanctuary of the mission. As kids are, we had to work around their 'energy.' Thank God Sister Angie and my wife Sandra assisted me in this venture. The rehearsals went well, and in time we were invited to sing at a church in Brooklyn. Back in the day, song writing came very easily to me, and so, I created a composition for the group. We sang our first debut song in the church, and it went very well. However, not long after singing my original composition in a church we visited, I had dropped off one of our new member Sister Cheryl Ledlum at a location in East New York and was startled when I heard 'my song,' the one that I had just wrote for the Youth Choir being sung by another group. Not only did it scare me, but it reemphasized to me the need that artists must always copyright their original creation, that way no one else can steal it. Unfortunately, our youth choir did not last long. Two of the children had an internal 'squabbling' with each other, then shortly after that, everything folded. Unfortunately, I was never able to get everyone back. However, from my experiences at the Pacific Street Mission, they were sharpening me to forge ahead despite temporary setbacks.

FOOD DISTRIBUTION ON PACIFIC STREET AND THE BLOCK ASSOCIATION PRESIDENT

As we have done for our Christmas and Thanksgiving outreach, the effort to collect and distribute mostly non-perishable items continued several times in the neighborhood. On one occasion, folks from the neighborhood came inside of the building, picked up the bags that were prepared for them and proceeded to make a 'beeline' to the exit door. However, in that instance, I had stopped them from leaving, had a word of prayer and informed them that we were in the community to assist in whatever way possible. I did not want a 'grab-n-go' response from folks. They needed to know that great efforts went into preparing the gift bags for them.

One would think that a free food giveaway would be a sure thing; it wasn't! But what I did not state was the fact that I had to go and compel the residents in one of the apartment buildings by knocking on their doors to remind them that the mission had prepared gift bags for them. It was a bit frustrating dealing with the mentality of some of our people, even when you'd prepared a blessing for them.

In my effort to further engraft myself into the community, I made several attempts to find out who the block association president was, and where I could find the person? My inquiries always ended up in a dead-end, until one day a woman approached me with an attitude. I discovered that she was the block association president. (However,) I was dumbfounded by the statement that she made when we met. She stated that, "I was trying to take over;" whether she meant her position, or the neighborhood, I really did not know. I just found it strange that trying to reach out to the neighbors and do something positive in the neighborhood caused such friction in that person's life. I think that as time passed on, we briefly spoke peaceably with each other. The encounter I had with that person started abruptly but thank God it ended peacefully. Even though I did not get a chance to work with her, the work in the Pacific Street Mission continued. My position remained; I did not volunteer to go to Pacific Street to work with a disgruntled block association president, I went there to minister to the community. There were many other ideas that were surging in my spirit that had to come out, and I was determined to pursue them.

CREATED MUSICAL CONCERTS

Being involved in photography, I've always taken note of how things are arranged; what is in the foreground, background, whether a subject is centered, how to use space for placing lettering and so on. I've also made it a study to learn how flyers are arranged, and whether they are eye-catching or boring. I should also state here that it was important for me to know who my targeted audience was. I made several attempts to learn the science of how to be selective in pursuing a targeted demographic. Several ideas were implemented to draw attention to our mission. One of them was to put on concerts. I enlisted the help of some of our singing folks from our main church and sent out invites to a few groups to see whether they wanted to participate. The internet was another source that was used to broaden my appeal. I thought, "Why do all the leg work by going from 'pillar to post,' let the internet do the walking." I used that medium plus the mailing system to search and reach all the colleges in the tri-state area and targeted their Student Affairs Department. It was and still is the same tactic used by advertisers when they are targeting a certain demographic or when they are attempting to promote and push a product. Whether it was the right department to send the flyers to, I did not care, I was casting a broad net.

As I have mentioned about photography, I used my God given talent to create flyers that were eye catching, colorful and attractive. With each concert we gave, the ticket price was always the same, $5.00. Though cheap, I wanted to get the most participation I could with an inexpensive entry admission fee. Another approach that was used was using our broadcast on WWRL to promote the concerts. Flyers were given out to membership for them to post around their neighborhoods, and of course, promotion by word of mouth was used to build up excitement.

What caught my attention from one of our concerts was the response I heard from one of the participants. The person stated that they thought they were coming to a big established church by the flyer they had received. In other words, by the professional look of the flyer, that person was moved to believe that the place, or the church they were going to was one with a steeple, a Hammond organ and a mass choir. Little did they know that they were invited to come into our brick building to sing and have church with us. So, I think one of the lessons I learned from that experience was not to think small, but to think big. Not to plan small, but to plan big. Not to short-change the Lord, but to challenge my faith into believing that "I can do all things through Christ who strengthens me." One lesson each leader needs to come to grips with is having the ability to 'envision on a large scale.' If fear and doubt are present, tackle them, master them and put them aside. Leadership must have the vision to envision great possibilities, ventures and endeavors. Consider for a moment the scripture found in Ez. 37:1-10 "The hand of the LORD came upon me, and he brought me out by the spirit of the LORD and set me down in the middle of a valley; it was full of bones. He led me all around them; there were very many lying in the valley, and they were very dry. He said to me, "Mortal, can these bones live?" I answered, "O Lord GOD, you know." Then he said to me, "Prophesy to these bones, and say to them: O dry bones, hear the word of the LORD. Thus says the Lord GOD to these bones: I will cause breath to enter you, and you shall live. I will lay sinews on you, and will cause flesh to come upon you, and cover you with skin, and put breath in you, and you shall live; and you shall know that I am the LORD." So I prophesied as I had been commanded; and as I prophesied, suddenly there was a noise, a rattling, and the bones came together, bone to its bone. I looked, and there were sinews on them, and flesh had come upon them, and skin had covered them; but there was no breath in them. Then he said to me, "Prophesy to the breath, prophesy, mortal, and say to the breath: Thus says the Lord GOD: Come from the four winds, O breath, and breathe upon these slain, that they may live." I prophesied as he commanded me, and the breath came into them, and they lived, and stood on their feet, a vast multitude."God placed his servant in a valley that looked 'hopeless.' He placed him in a situation that looked insurmountable and desolate and then asked what seemed to most people a crazy question. However, the lesson here is not to think small. With God on our side, no challenge, obstacle or failures should stop us from achieving our goals.

DISTRICT COOK-OUT

I have included the District Cook-Out in this segment because it is closely associated with my tenure and the lessons learned while I was pastoring at the Pacific Street Mission. Early on in my writings, I stated that I don't know where the spirit of tenacity came from. Looking back through the years, I saw that much of what I did was done in that spirit. Plainly put, back then I used to say, "Let's try it and see what happens." In my developing years, I witnessed too many 'failures' and 'inconsistencies' around me. So, that may have been one of the reasons why the Lord instilled that tenacious spirit within me. I did not back down from assignments, but with each, challenged myself to go and grow even higher. I did not wait for the next person to raise their hands, but at times, I had mine up before anyone else did.

I remember planning for our District Cook-Out back in the day. I purposely did not call it a "pick-nic" because of the association of blacks being hung from trees while white spectators came to watch a public hanging. From what I understand, that is where the word came from. So, when planning our District Cook-Out, I had approached several members of our main church and 'told' them that they were to work with me in organizing and planning the event. I don't believe I gave them a chance to accept or decline, I simply 'told' them to help me, and thank God they did. What I felt back then (*and still do now*), was that too many of us (*black folks in general*), did not step up to the plate and assume responsibility. Now, I'm sure that response travels through all ethnic groups, but too many of us give up the mantle of responsibility because we are either afraid, don't want to be challenged, don't like to be put 'on the carpet' or simply would rather have someone else assume the responsibility. To accomplish this monumental task of organizing a cook-out, calling and renting a bus for the trip, buying all food stuff, developing games for folks to engage in, getting tickets sold, organizing the additional membership to help bag all articles and praying for a sunny and successful day, I 'told' and appointed several people to assist me. Two of the people that I approached were Sisters Pam Williams and Darlene Bryant. Both sisters, though demure in nature, rolled up their sleeves and helped me tremendously in accomplishing our goal. Some others, such as Robert Knowing, Min. Dorothy Isaac, Deacon Rosa Potts and my wife Sandra, were also helpful in organizing the event.

When the event took place, we could not have had a more perfect day to fellowship together. Both church and non-church members came out and everyone had a great time. I was very glad to capture the success of our District Cook-Out on motion film. I was also pleased with capturing some of the saints who went on to meet the Lord as well as my mother who also attended and participated. Unfortunately, we made one misjudgment in our calculations. We had purchased too much food for the event. On arrival back at the church, we gave much of it away to anyone who wanted it. But overall, the event was a complete success, and everyone enjoyed themselves!

CREATED A PHOTOGRAPHY CLUB

Looking back in retrospect, I believe it was Sister Pat Oduba from our main church (415 Atlantic Ave.) who donated a few film cameras. As God has blessed me with a number of talents, I took a liking to the art of photography from a very young age. And through the years, I've sharpened the art to know what a 'good shot' is from what wasn't. I supposed that from all of the pictures I was taking inside and outside of the church, it caught the attention of one of our members. One day, Sister Pat Oduba approached me and asked whether I could use some old Instamatic film cameras. Of course, my answer was "yes." So soon after that, she bestowed upon me approximately 5 to 6 instamatic cameras. So, as time went on, I decided to start a photography club with some of the youth in our church. The participants were: Sister Chyann, Sister Hadijah and Sister Nicole. Some film was purchased, instructions given out, and we found ourselves walking from the church to Prospect Park to take some pictures. I must say, the young ladies did very well in their picture taking. Please keep in mind, cell phones were not as prevalent during that time. They did not have the training to take decent shots that most people get when they repeatedly use their cell phone cameras. So, to take a good or great shot was a 'biggie.' However, during our time in Prospect Park, a local politician came through the park with reporters asking questions. I then instructed the girls to 'get the shot.' I wanted them to learn how to 'position themselves' to get the ideal shot. And if it meant "pressing your way into the crowd," then so be it; get the shot. Some of those techniques I've developed through the years of photography. Techniques such as: finding the right angle, anticipating the next move, being ready to shoot, and pressing my way through a crowd to get the shot were all developed through the years of photography. So, as instructed, they pressed their way to 'get the shot.' I suppose one lesson that can be learned here is that to get what you are after, one has to have the guts and boldness to jump in the mix and at times, force their way to get what they are after. Too many times many may feel a slight embarrassment or even fear in taking some risks. But if anyone wants to achieve their goal, it may require a certain tenacity and perseverance to achieve it. Hopefully after the experience in the park, the three young ladies learned a valuable lesson on pressing their way to 'get the shot.'

GOOD FRIDAY PRESENTATIONS

I do not recall whether the Good Friday Presentations started while I was in the position of Pioneer Minister at the Pacific Street Mission, or whether I was already in the position of Northeast District Minister. However, the Good Friday services were originally done by Sr. Min. Alice Edwards and eventually, it was transferred over to me. I suppose my creative side took over again when I started looking at what could be done with the services. It has always been a thought of mine not to follow in 'traditions, customs, and rituals' when it came to ministry and sharing the Word of God. I think too often, something is lost when anyone does that. Someone once said, "Familiarity breeds contempt." Not only is that true, but it also applies to the gospel of Jesus Christ. Take for instance, when the word of God states, "Behold, I will do a new thing; now it shall spring forth; shall ye not know it? I will even make a way in the wilderness, *and* rivers in the desert" (Isa 43:19); how does one interpret that? So, I moved away from the traditional way the service had been presented. I took a different approach and injected the creative side of my nature into the services; hence, the Good Friday Presentations were born.

Putting on the services involved tapping into the many years spent in observing, learning, critiquing, questioning, envisioning, challenging doubts and fears, reaching outside of the 'box,' leading, directing and challenging people to go beyond their perceived limitations, believing and trusting God for success of the ventures, arriving early and oftentimes leaving late, sacrificing time, confronting and interviewing people on the street, taping employees on my job, going 'in pocket' to purchase equipment that was needed, advertising and promoting the event, rehearsing with participants, writing scripts and so on and so on. My point here is to state that leadership involves a certain level of 'tenacity,' 'determination,' 'perseverance,' 'consistency' and 'commitment' to move forward. While others are resting or sleeping, leadership must always be ready to sacrifice time and energy for the cause. Also, in every presentation that was done for our Good Friday services, I wanted to leave a 'challenging thought' with the audience. A thought that would have us take a closer look. I wanted us to look at how church and ministry is viewed by the outside world; were we being effective enough in disseminating the gospel of Jesus Christ, or were we just a glorified club? I was concerned about the relationship that Christ spoke about when He stated, "A new commandment I give unto you, that ye love one another; as I have loved you, that ye also love one another" (John 13:34). We also tapped into the traditional approach which is normally done during Good Friday service. So, I also enlisted the services and participation of our youth, deacons, ministers, and pastors to render the Seven Last Words of Christ.

I certainly could not go on without mentioning two people who were extremely instrumental in assisting me with all the Good Friday presentations that we did. The two sacrificial angels were Sister Darlene Bryant and Sr. Min. Gloria Daniels. Those two sisters hung in there with me through it all. As I think of them, one held up my right arm, and the other my left. They shared their time and energy in helping to get the job done. I will eternally be grateful for the love they have shared in helping to organize and follow through with each presentation.

EXTERNAL MINISTRIES

As I am coming to the end of my writing, I think it would be wise for me to interject what helped to shape my thought process early on in ministry. I thank God that during my life, growing up in Colon Panama, I was brought to this country by my mom, but led here by the Spirit of God. And in time, I spent learning and observing what was going on around me. Till the call of ministry came my way. Upon accepting the call, a certain 'seriousness' to the gospel of Christ took hold of me to the point that what I read, learned, and understood, shaped my thoughts then until now. I supposed it was at that point where I started asking questions to certain verses and stories that I read in the scriptures. Questions not for me to doubt and fall out of faith, but questions to pursue a deeper revelation and understanding of the gospel.

What I saw then in some churches was the resemblance of a 'club.' Within its walls, congregants came for several reasons. Either to show off their fashion apparel, shop for a husband or wife, showcase their musical abilities, or fleece the flock while gasping for breath when preaching. Certainly not all churches were of such individuals, but there were many of them that followed that pattern.

The other thing that caught my attention was the practices of certain churches. With some, I did not see the correlation of the teachings of scripture within their ministries. In other words, when it came to social and political issues, there was a great divide. The attention was geared more toward raising large sums of money for the preacher, having a colorful 100 voice choir or an edifice large enough to seat a thousand people. Issues of housing, education, garbage collection, adequate food in the community, unemployment, police injustice, political corruption were not written into the Sunday sermon of some of those preachers. Instead, greater emphasis was placed on the level of the pastor's anniversary and offering(s). So early on in ministry, I started reading and searching through the scriptures, and when I came upon certain verses, the questions came. For instance, on the onset of Jesus' ministry, the scroll was given to Him and He found the place where it was written, "The Spirit of the Lord *is* upon me, because he hath anointed me to preach the gospel to the poor; He hath sent me to heal the brokenhearted, to preach deliverance to the captives, and recovering of sight to the blind, to set at liberty them that are bruised, To preach the acceptable year of the Lord." (Luke 4:18-19) When I read those verses, the questions came; "Are we seeing that type of boldness in our churches?" Or take for instance another portion of scripture found in the gospel of Matt. 25:31-46. "When the Son of Man comes in his glory, and all the angels with him, then he will sit on the throne of his glory. All the nations will be gathered before him, and he will separate people one from another as a shepherd separates the sheep from the goats, and he will put the sheep at his right hand and the goats at the left. Then the king will say to those at his right hand, 'Come, you that are blessed by my Father, inherit the kingdom prepared for you from the foundation of the world; for I was hungry and you gave me food, I was thirsty and you gave me something to drink, I was a stranger and you welcomed me, I was naked and you gave me clothing, I was sick and you took care of me, I was in prison and you visited me.' Then the righteous will answer him, 'Lord, when was it that we saw you hungry and gave you food, or thirsty and gave you something to drink? And when was it that we saw you a stranger and welcomed you, or naked and gave you clothing? And when was it that we saw you sick or in prison and visited you?' And the king will answer them, 'Truly I tell you, just as you did it to one of the least of these who are members of my family, you did it to me.' Then he will say to those at his left hand, 'You that are accursed, depart from me into the eternal fire prepared for the devil and his angels; for I was hungry and you gave me no food, I was thirsty and you gave me nothing to drink, I was a stranger and you did not welcome me, naked and you did not give me clothing, sick and in prison and you did not visit me.' Then they also will answer, 'Lord, when was it that we saw you hungry or thirsty or a stranger or naked or sick or in prison, and did not take care of you?' Then he will answer them, 'Truly I tell you, just as you did not do it to one of the least of these, you did not do it to me.' And these will go away into eternal punishment, but the righteous into eternal life." Within those verses you will find two types of people, two types of ministries. One that empathizes and engages with the needs and suffering of people and another that doesn't. One who took on the character of Christ and 'naturally' ministered to people, and the other that was void of compassion and care. Some can 'hoop-n-holla' on a Sunday when the preacher gasps for his/her breath. Some can even 'clear a path' to showcase their 'shouting steps.' But preach a message like in Amos 5:24: "But let justice roll down like waters, and righteousness like an ever-flowing stream" then see how many 'get happy.' I dare say, not too many will shout behind a sermon like that.

I'm grateful that early on in ministry, I embraced the Mission Statement of our church. I'm also grateful that I saw the correlation of the Mission Statement intertwined with the teachings of scripture and the ministry of Christ. So, I started developing a critical eye as I viewed what some were and were not doing. I was privileged to participate in the Downtown boycott that attempted to bring attention and a voice to the unlawful killing of Randy Evans. I found myself first asking, "If Jesus was here (in the flesh), where would you find Him, and what would His ministry entail?"

Well, one does not need to go too far for an answer. Jesus' ministry would continue as it did in scripture - "Just then some Pharisees came to Jesus and said, "Go away from here and hide. Herod wants to kill you!" Jesus said to them, "Go tell that fox, Today and tomorrow I am forcing demons out of people and finishing my work of healing. Then, the next day, the work will be finished." Luke 13:31-32 There are numerous verses in the Word of God where Jesus and His disciples embodied the spirit of the 'prophets' as they confronted and challenged those in the seat of power. There was no dichotomy between engaging in social, church, political, Bible study, educational, unemployment or tarry service. The 'gospel' encompasses them all. So, I found myself not only embracing the tri-fold approaches of Jesus ministry (preaching, teaching, and healing), but also engaging in challenges outside the walls of the church building. I also understood that not everyone is called in one direction to voice their concerns and opinions. So, I used the medium of the pen and paper to write to certain politicians to voice my concerns and opinions. I also used the airwaves to share my thoughts. My voice became an instrument to encourage and challenge friends and neighbors to participate in the electoral process. As a minister of the gospel of Jesus Christ, ministry meant engaging myself in whatsoever manner possible (in my area of the vineyard), and not being afraid to go outside of the boundaries of that which felt familiar to me. So, when Arthur Eve ran for the mayorship of Buffalo and the church went to support him, our involvement fell right in line with how I came to understand the scriptures. When Sydenham Hospital in Harlem was on the verge of closing, our church held a sit-in outside its borders to keep the building open. When Mayor Ed Koch loudly paraded down Atlantic Avenue, we drove him away and forced him to respond to police brutality. We also found ourselves in Manhattan demonstrating in front of Jimmy Carter when he came there for a political function. But just as we've participated in addressing the ills of the land, it was also an honor for me to participate and support David Dinkins when he ran and succeeded as the first Black Mayor of New York, and Jesse Jackson when he ran for the presidency of the United States. Again, within my mind, there was no dichotomy involved. 'Church and state' stood as a single entity that I/we engage ourselves in. The Christ of God was big enough to carry to a political, educational, demonstration or a revival service. Yet, in retrospect, I'm grateful to have participated and learned the doctrine of The House of the Lord Church and its leader the Rev. Dr. Herbert D. Daughtry. As a young minister back in the Pacific Street era, I believe I have garnered much experience to not only feel confident addressing most of the issues of our times, but to also engraft them into the preached Word on a Sunday morning. And now, several years later, I have been able to use those experiences to benefit and enrich the congregation I now pastor.

www.ingramcontent.com/pod-product-compliance
Lightning Source LLC
Chambersburg PA
CBHW051232120626
46547CB00013B/1609